Names of Jesus
A, B, C's

Names of Jesus A, B, C's

Written by Steve Newby

Illustrated by Carolyn Holmes

XULON PRESS

Xulon Press Elite
2301 Lucien Way #415
Maitland, FL 32751
407.339.4217
www.xulonpress.com

Xulon ELITE

© 2019 by Steve Newby

All rights reserved solely by the author. The author guarantees all contents are original and do not infringe upon the legal rights of any other person or work. No part of this book may be reproduced in any form without the permission of the author. The views expressed in this book are not necessarily those of the publisher.

Unless otherwise indicated, Scripture quotations taken from the English Standard Version (ESV). Copyright © 2001 by Crossway, a publishing ministry of Good News Publishers. Used by permission. All rights reserved.

Printed in the United States of America.

ISBN-13: 978-1-6305-0907-1

Dedication

Dedicated to courageous Christian families in countries where parents are forbidden by government to teach their children about Jesus. A portion of the proceeds from this book will go to Voice of the Martyrs, an organization which serves the persecuted church worldwide.

Introduction for Parents

The Holy Bible contains over a hundred names and titles for the Lord Jesus Christ. Each name highlights a different aspect of His Person and work. His names declare that Jesus is the eternal God of creation Who came into the world as a baby born to a Virgin, lived a sinless life, revealed to us the Father, and performed miracles of healing, deliverance, and resurrection. He perfectly fulfilled the Law's righteous demands and the Old Testament messianic types and prophecies. Then, out of love, Jesus voluntarily gave His life as the full and sufficient representative and substitutionary sacrifice for the sin of humanity. He rose from the grave victorious over sin, death, and hell, and ascended into heaven. After a series of clearly-prophesied events, He will return with those who have believed in Him to rule the earth as King of kings. Finally, Jesus Christ will give to His own the eternal home in the new heaven and new earth He has prepared for them.

This little book presents names of Jesus beginning with each letter of the English alphabet. For some letters there are multiple names, such as for "L" – Lamb of God, Light of the world, Lion of Judah, Lord, Lord of lords, and others. There are no obvious names of Jesus beginning with some letters of the English alphabet — Q, U, X, and Z, for example. In these and some other cases, biblical terms describing Christ are given instead of proper names.

While some truths about Christ are beyond the grasp of children of alphabet-learning age (and adults, too, for that matter), youngsters can and do develop a wonder and reverence for God and His Word at very early ages. The Lord Jesus holds up the faith and humility of children as an example for all. "Truly, I say to you, whoever does not receive the kingdom of God like a child shall not enter it." Mark 10:15.

Therefore God has highly exalted him and bestowed on him the name that is above every name, that at the name of Jesus every knee should bow, in heaven and on earth and under the earth, and every tongue confess that Jesus Christ is Lord, to the glory of God the Father. Philippians 2:9-11

And there is salvation in no one else, for there is no other name under heaven given among men by which we must be saved. Acts 4:12

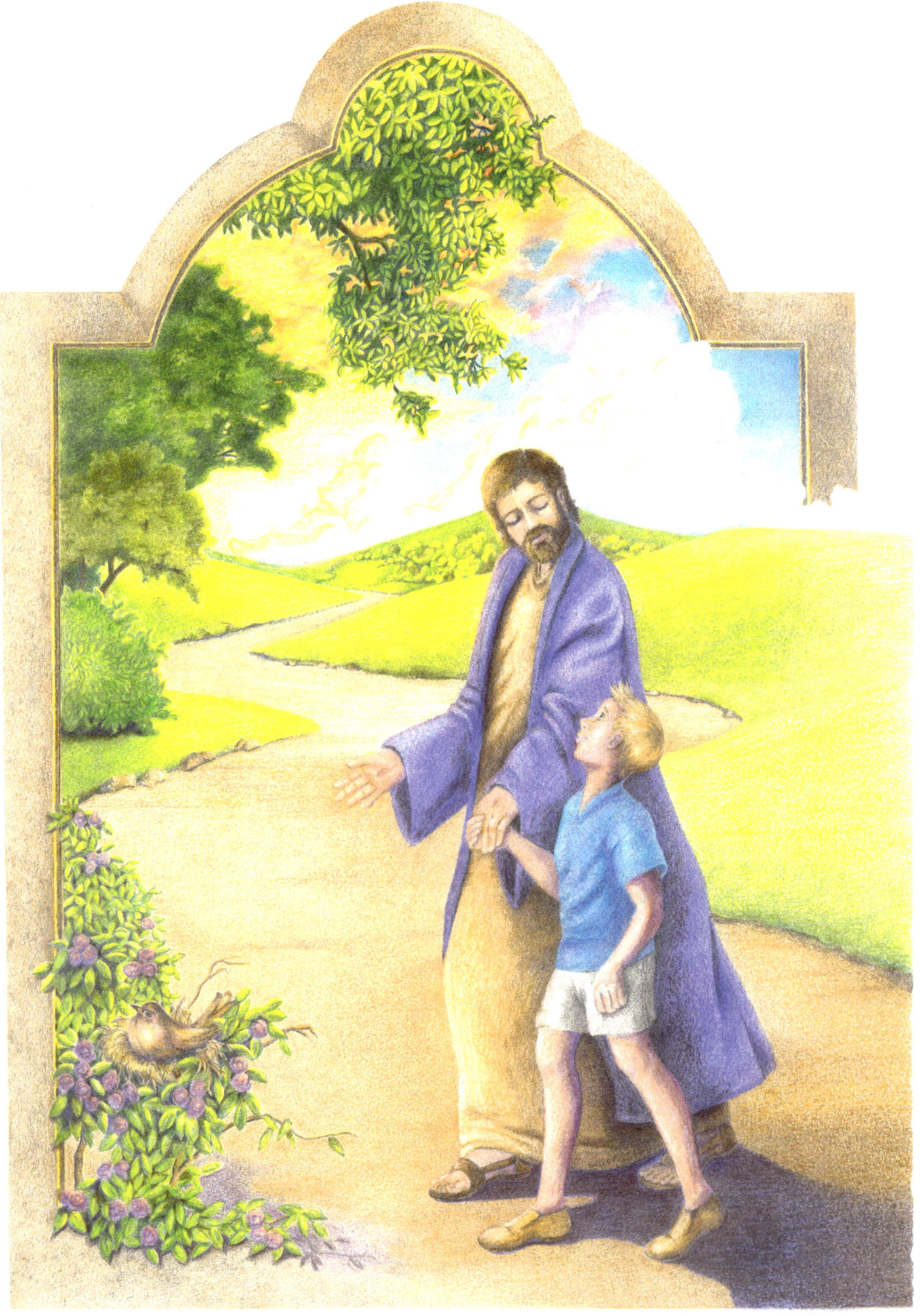

Alpha and Omega,
the Beginning and the End;
Jesus lives forever;
He will always be my Friend.

———————

I am the Alpha and the Omega, the first and the last, the beginning and the end. Revelation 22:13

Fear not, I am the first and the last, and the living one. I died, and behold I am alive forevermore . . . Revelation 1:17-18

You are my friends if you do what I command you. No longer do I call you servants, for the servant does not know what his master is doing; but I have called you friends, for all that I have heard from my Father I have made known to you.

Alpha and Omega are the first and last letters of the Greek alphabet (like A and Z in English), the language in which the New Testament was written. This means that Jesus always was and will always be. He has no beginning or end. He IS the beginning and the end.

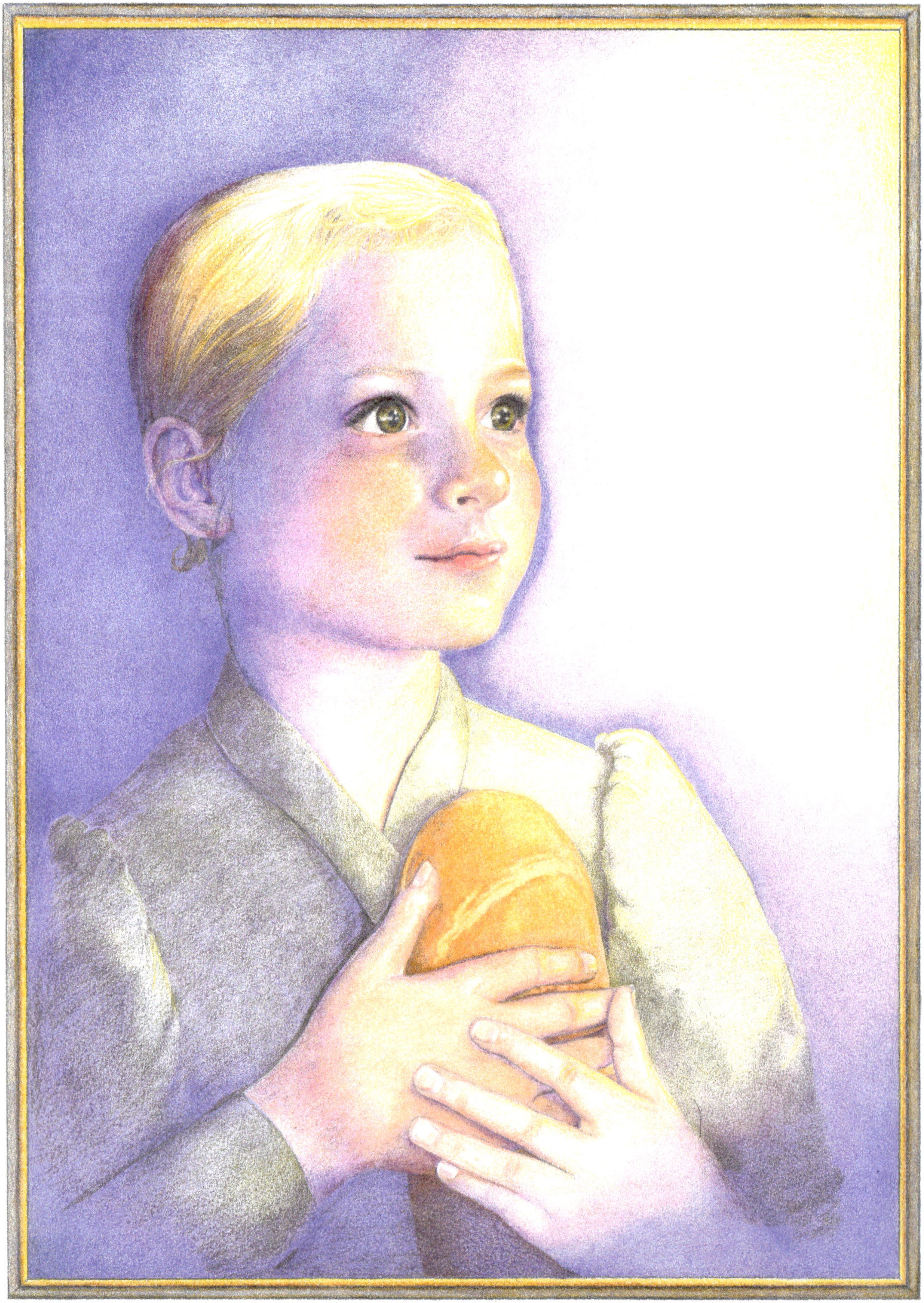

Beloved of the Father,
Jesus holds me in His hand;
He loves me as the Father loves,
and I love His command.
Jesus is the Bread of Life;
He is the Living Bread;
My trusting heart is satisfied
as by Him I am fed.

---

and behold, a voice from heaven said, "This is my beloved Son, with whom I am well pleased. Matthew 3:17.

The Father loves the Son and has given all things into his hand. John 3:35.

As the Father has loved me, so have I loved you. Abide in my love. If you keep my commandments, you will abide in my love, just as I have kept my Father's commandments and abide in his love. John 15:9-10

I am the bread of life. John 6:48.

I am the living bread that came down from heaven. John 6:51.

Jesus said to them, "I am the bread of life; whoever comes to me shall not hunger, and whoever believes in me shall never thirst. John 6:3

For he satisfies the longing soul, and the hungry soul he fills with good things. Psalms 107:9

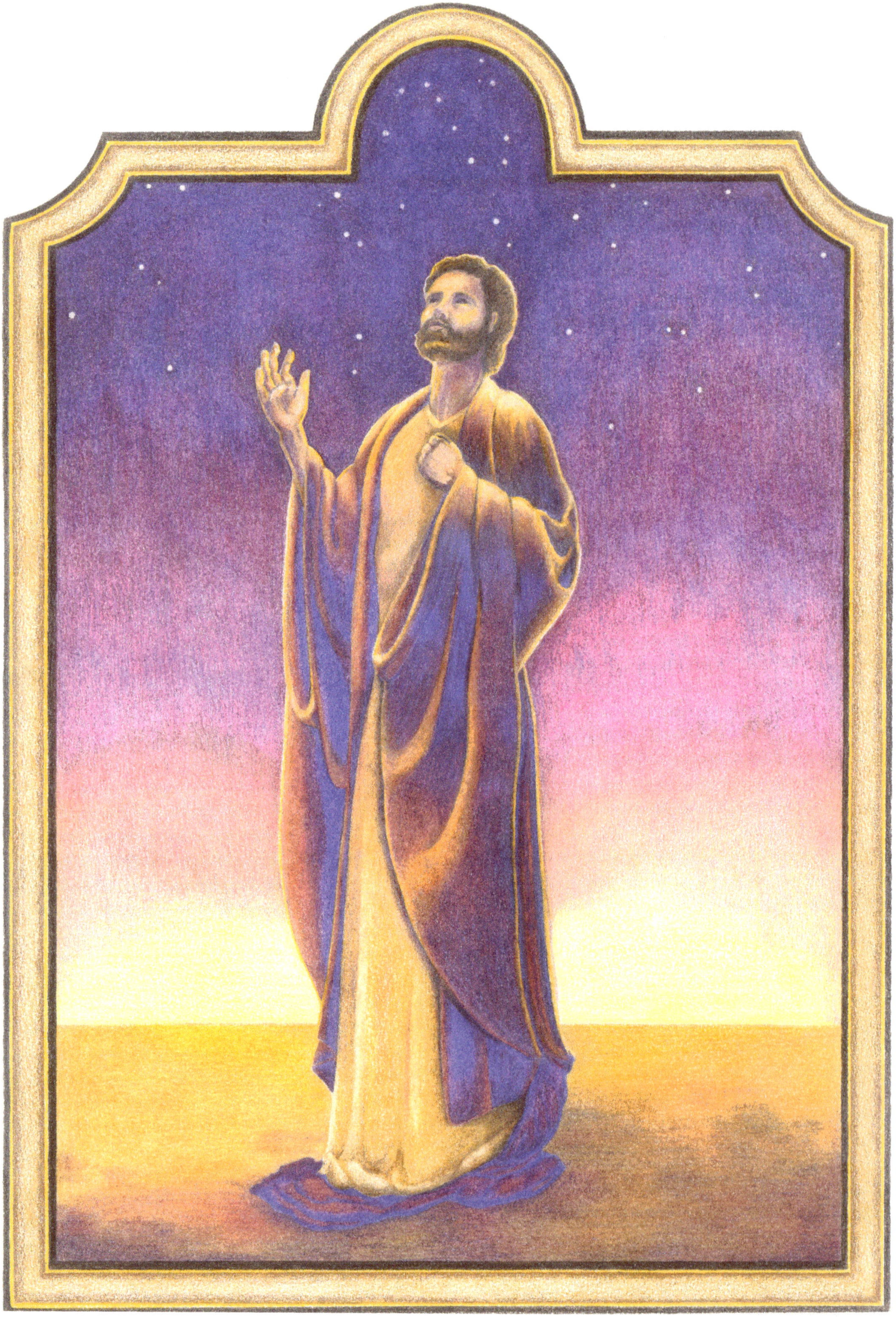

Christ is the Creator;
He made the earth and skies;
He spoke and they appeared;
He is powerful and wise.

By faith we understand that the universe was created by the word of God, so that what is seen was not made out of things that are visible. Hebrews 11:3

All things were made through him, and without him was not anything made that was made. John 1:3.

For by him all things were created, in heaven and on earth, visible and invisible . . . Colossians 1:16.

By the word of the LORD the heavens were made, and by the breath of his mouth all their host...For he spoke, and it came to be; he commanded, and it stood firm. Psalms 33:6,9.

The voice of the LORD is powerful; the voice of the LORD is full of majesty. Psalms 29:4

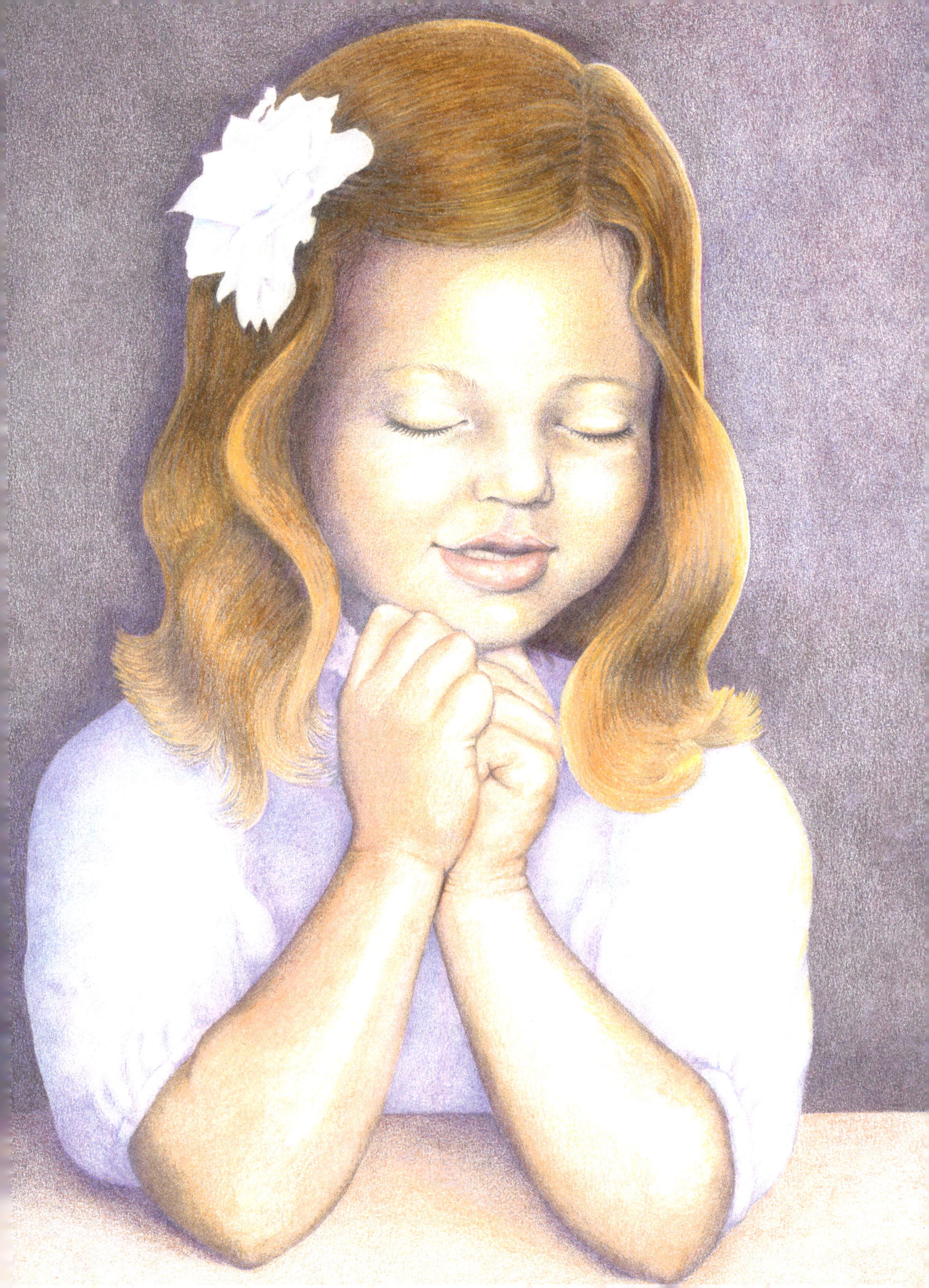

Jesus Christ is the Door,
the true and only Way;
I come to God by trusting Him;
He hears me when I pray.

I am the door. If anyone enters by me, he will be saved and will go in and out land find pasture. John 10:9.

Jesus said to him, "I am the way, the truth, and the life. No one comes to the Father except through me. John 14:6.

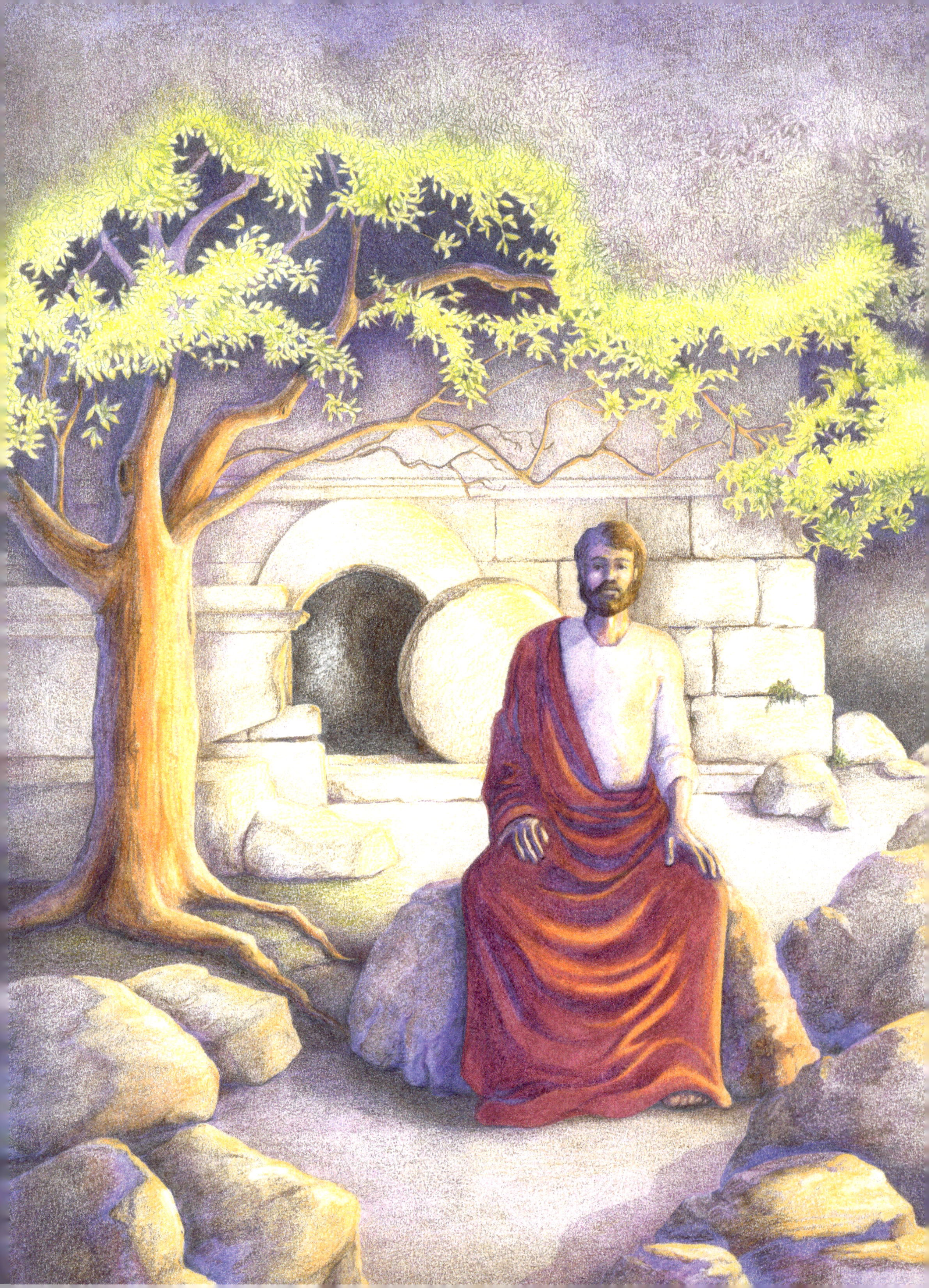

Christ is the Ever-Living One;
He rose up from the grave;
Everyone who calls on Him,
He promises to save.

―――――――

Wherefore he is able to save them to the uttermost that come unto God by him, seeing he ever liveth to make intercession for them. Hebrews 7:25, King James Version

We know that Christ, being raised from the dead, will never die again; death no longer has dominion over him. Romans 6:9

For everyone who calls on the name of the LORD will be saved. Romans 10:13.

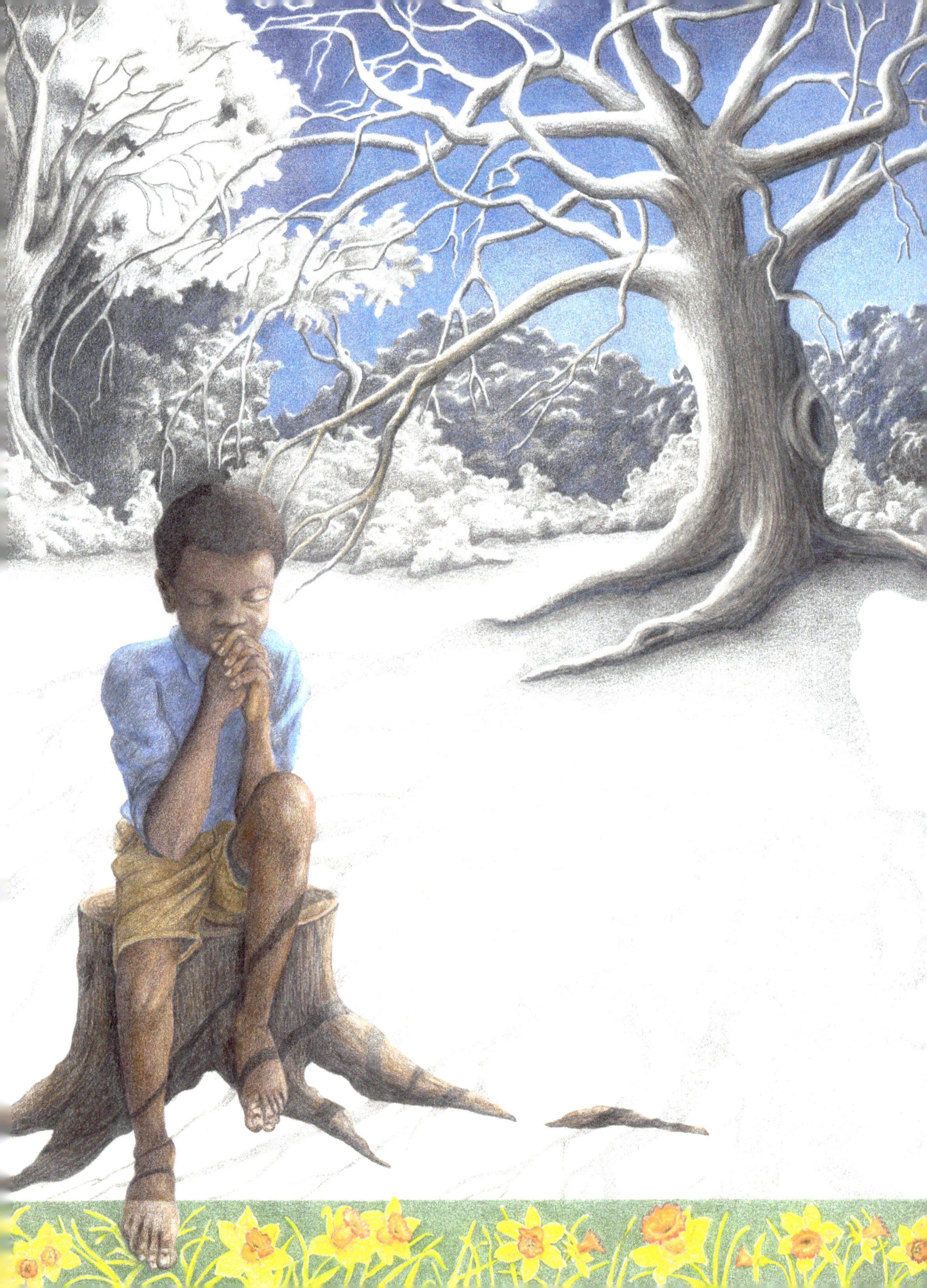

The First-Born from the dead is He,
Faithful and True;
He promises eternal life,
His gift to me and you.

. . . He is the beginning, the firstborn from the dead, that in everything he might be preeminent. Colossians 1:18.

Then I saw heaven opened, and behold, a white horse! The one sitting on it is called Faithful and True . . . Revelation 19:11

For the wages of sin is death, but the free gift of God is eternal life in Christ Jesus our Lord. Romans 6:23.

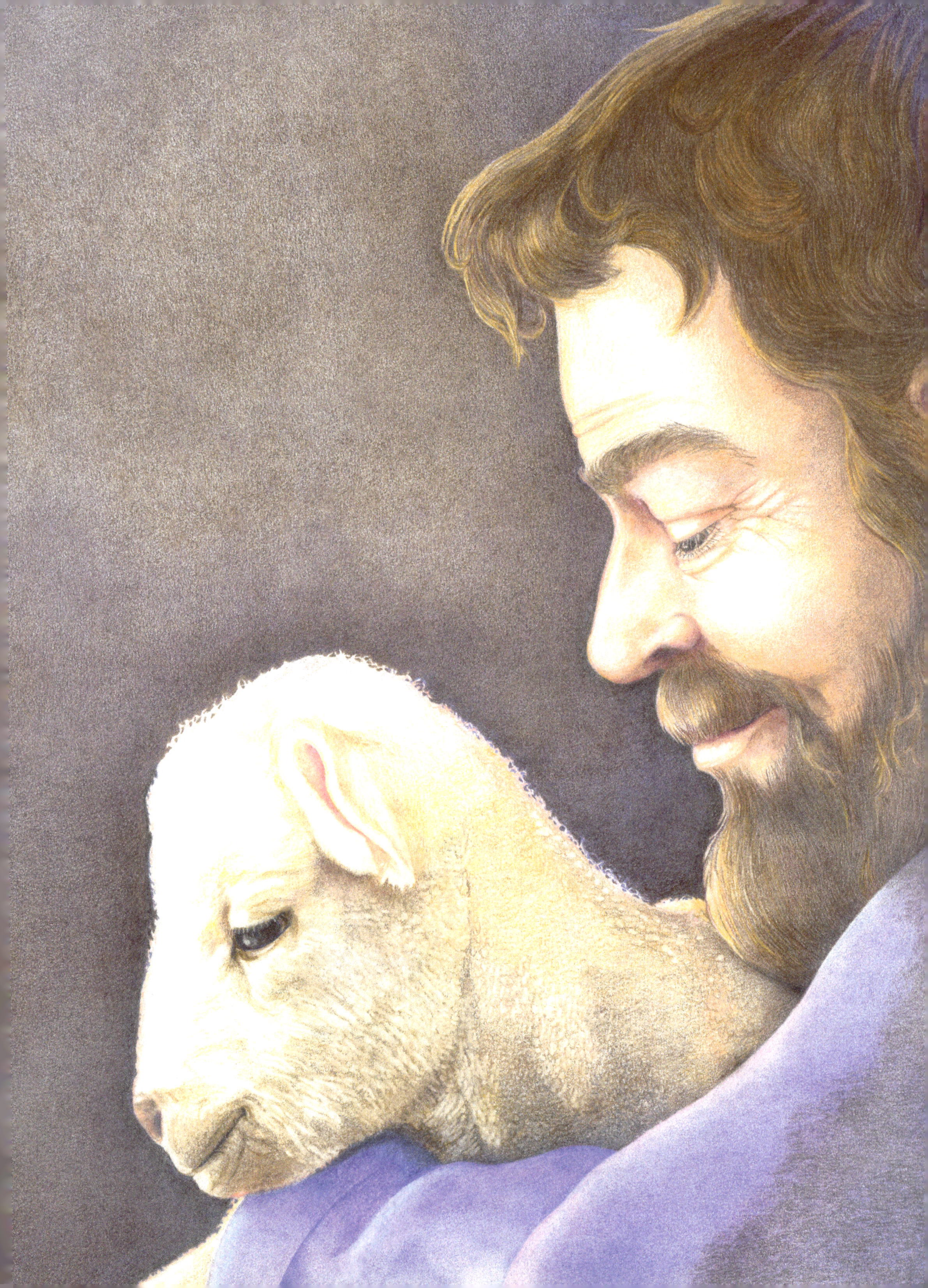

The **G**ood Shepherd knows and loves His sheep;

in Him I will rejoice;

His own He does protect and keep;

they hear and know His voice.

The **G**ood Shepherd knows and loves His sheep;

His little lamb am I;

He gives to me eternal life;

my soul will never die.

───────

I am the good shepherd. I know my own and my own know me. John 10:14.

My sheep hear my voice, and I know them, and they follow me. John 10:27

I am the good shepherd. I know my own and my own know me . . . I give them eternal life, and they will never perish, and no one is able to snatch them out of the Father's hand. John 10:27-28.

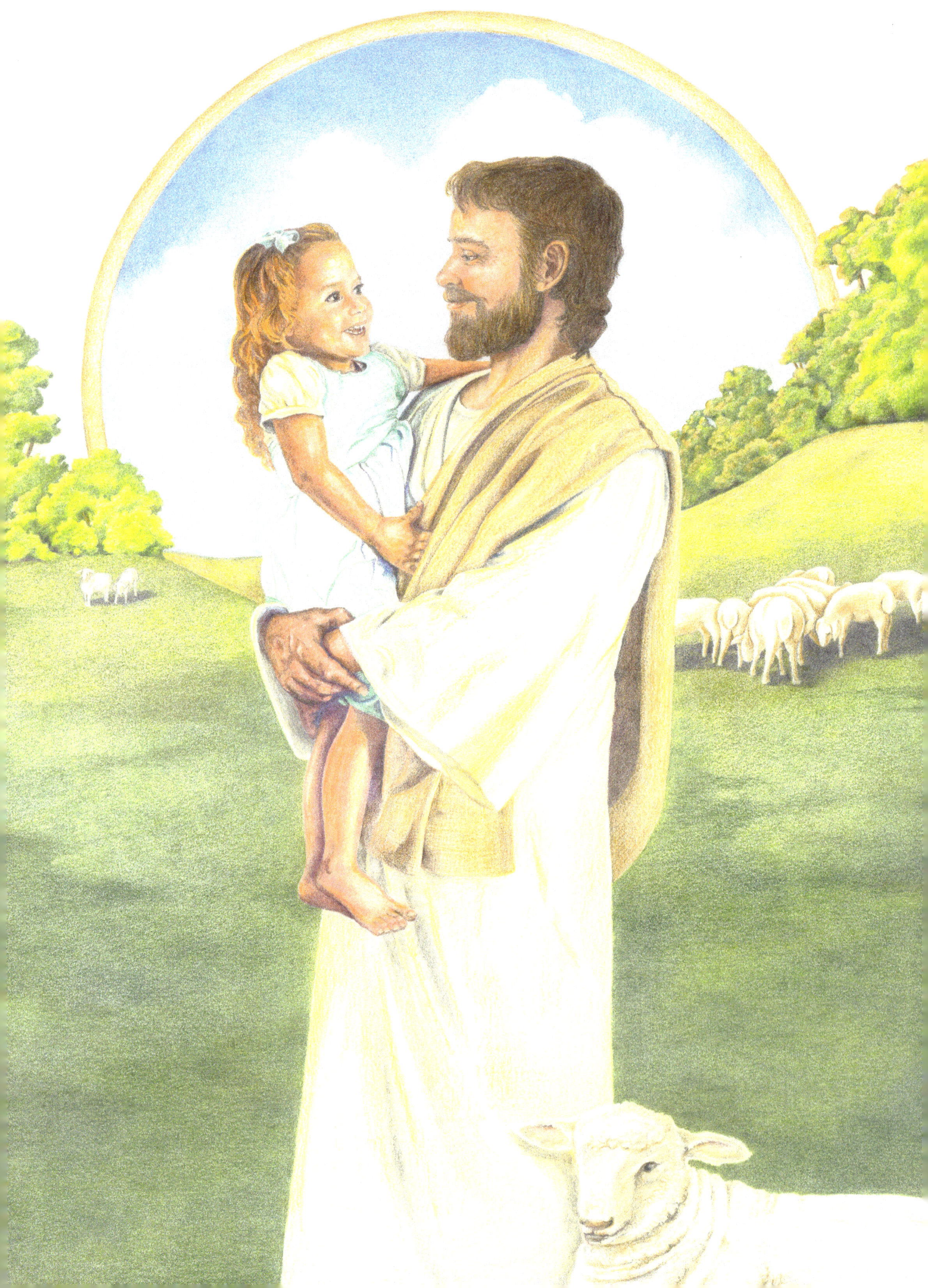

The Holy One is my High Priest,
blameless and pure;
Jesus is my Hope and joy;
His promises are sure.

. . . I know who you are – the Holy One of God. Mark 1:24.

For it was indeed fitting that we should have such a high priest, holy, innocent, unstained, separated from sinners, exalted above the heavens. Hebrews 7:26.

Paul, an apostle of Christ Jesus by command of God our Savior and of Christ Jesus our hope. Colossians 1:1.

. . . the testimony of the LORD is sure, making wise the simple. Psalms 19:7.

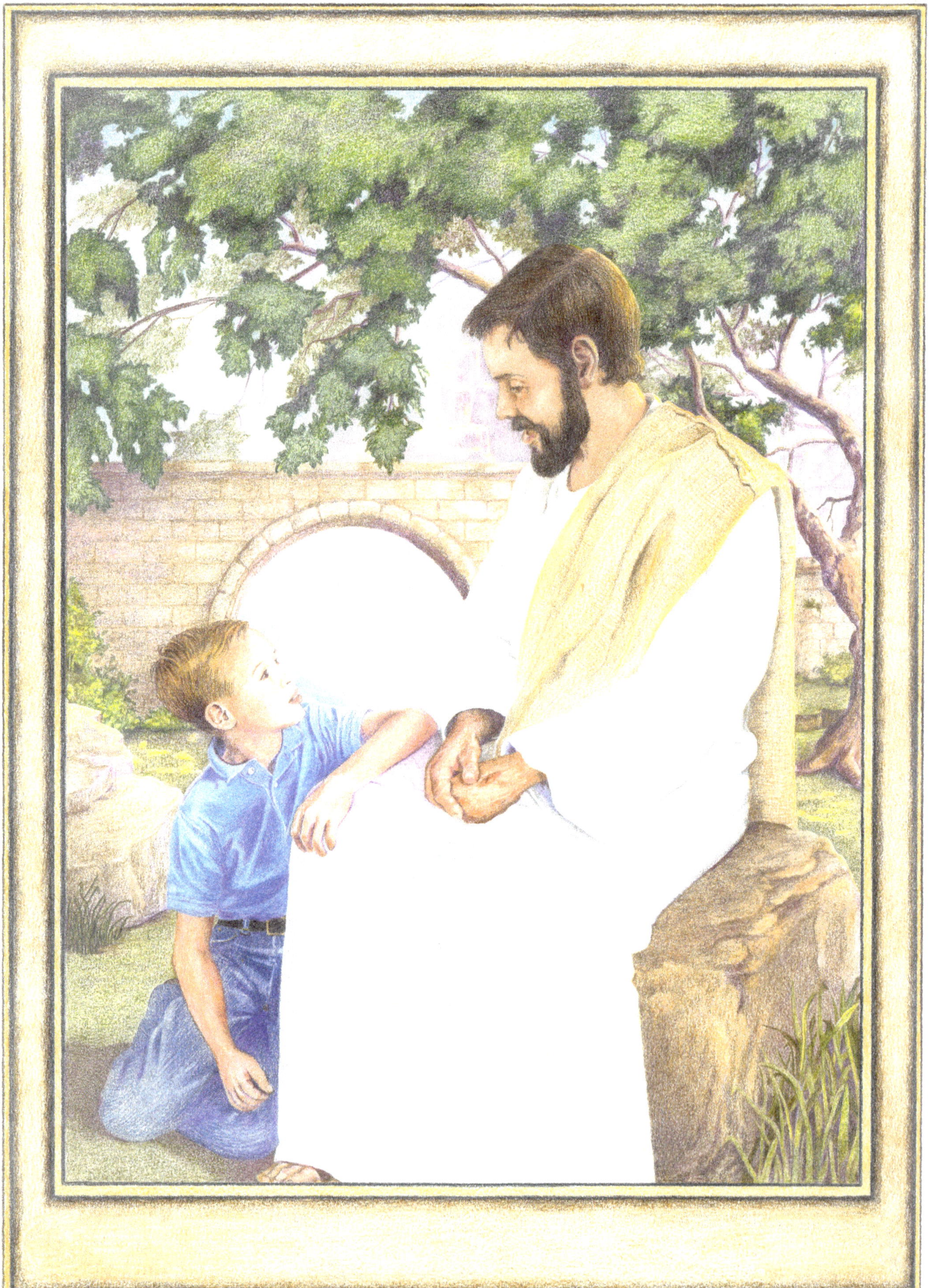

I Am – Jesus always was,
and always He will be;
Immanuel – God with us;
He came for you and me.

Jesus said to them, "Truly, truly, I say to you, before Abraham was, I am. John 8:58.

Behold the virgin shall conceive and bear a son, and they shall call his name Immanuel (which means, God with us). Matthew 1:23.

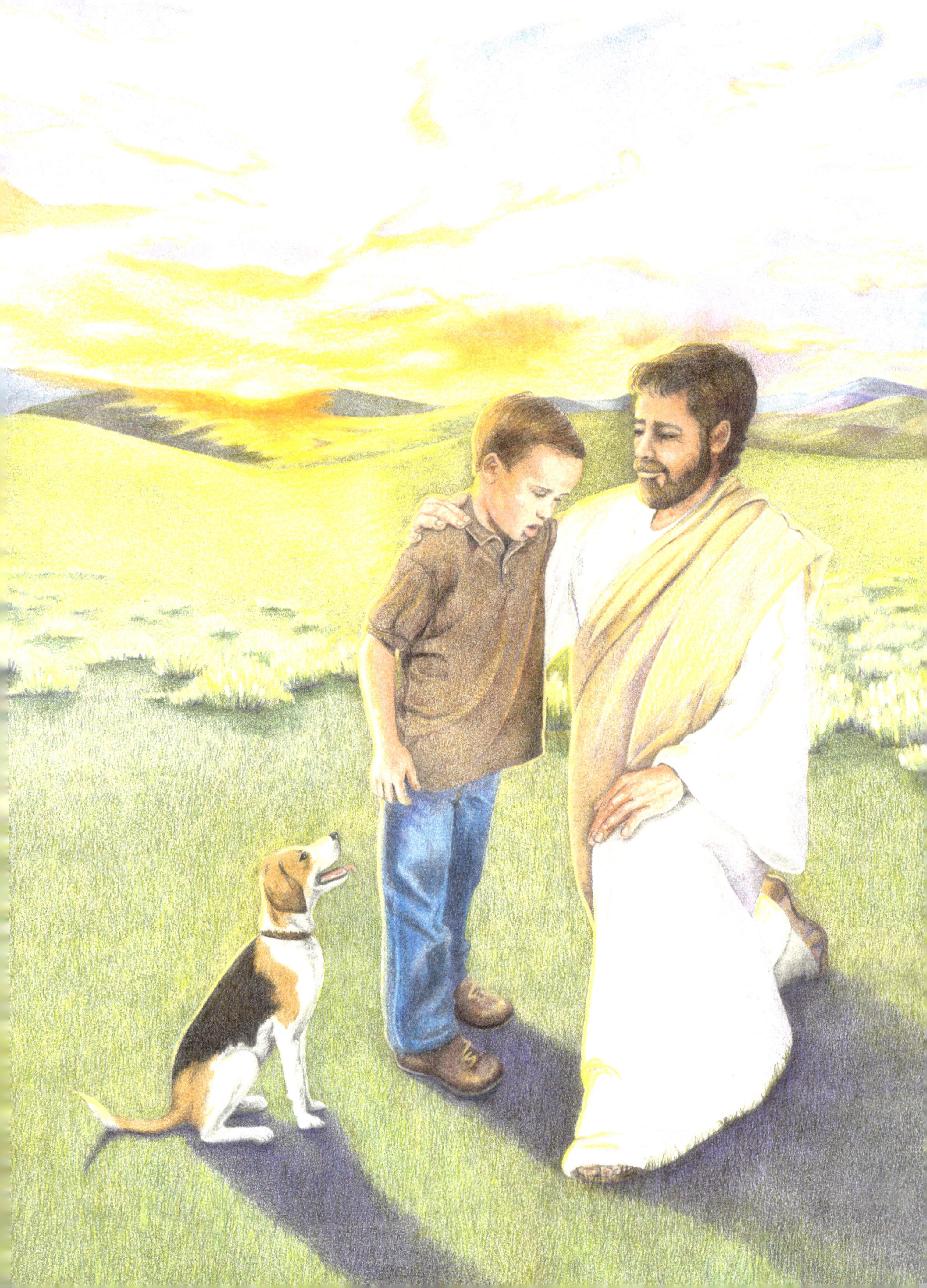

Jesus means, "**J**ehovah saves."
He saves me from my sin;
Eternal life He gives to all
who put their trust in Him.

She will bear a son and you shall call his name Jesus, for he will save his people from their sins. Matthew 1:21

Truly, truly, I say to you, whoever hears my word and believes him who sent me has eternal life. He does not come into judgment, but has passed from death to life. John 5:24.

Isaiah 6:1

His royal name is King of kings;
His rule is over all;
And yet He loves each little child;
it matters not how small.

———

On his robe and on his thigh he has a name written, King of kings and Lord of lords. Revelation 19:16.

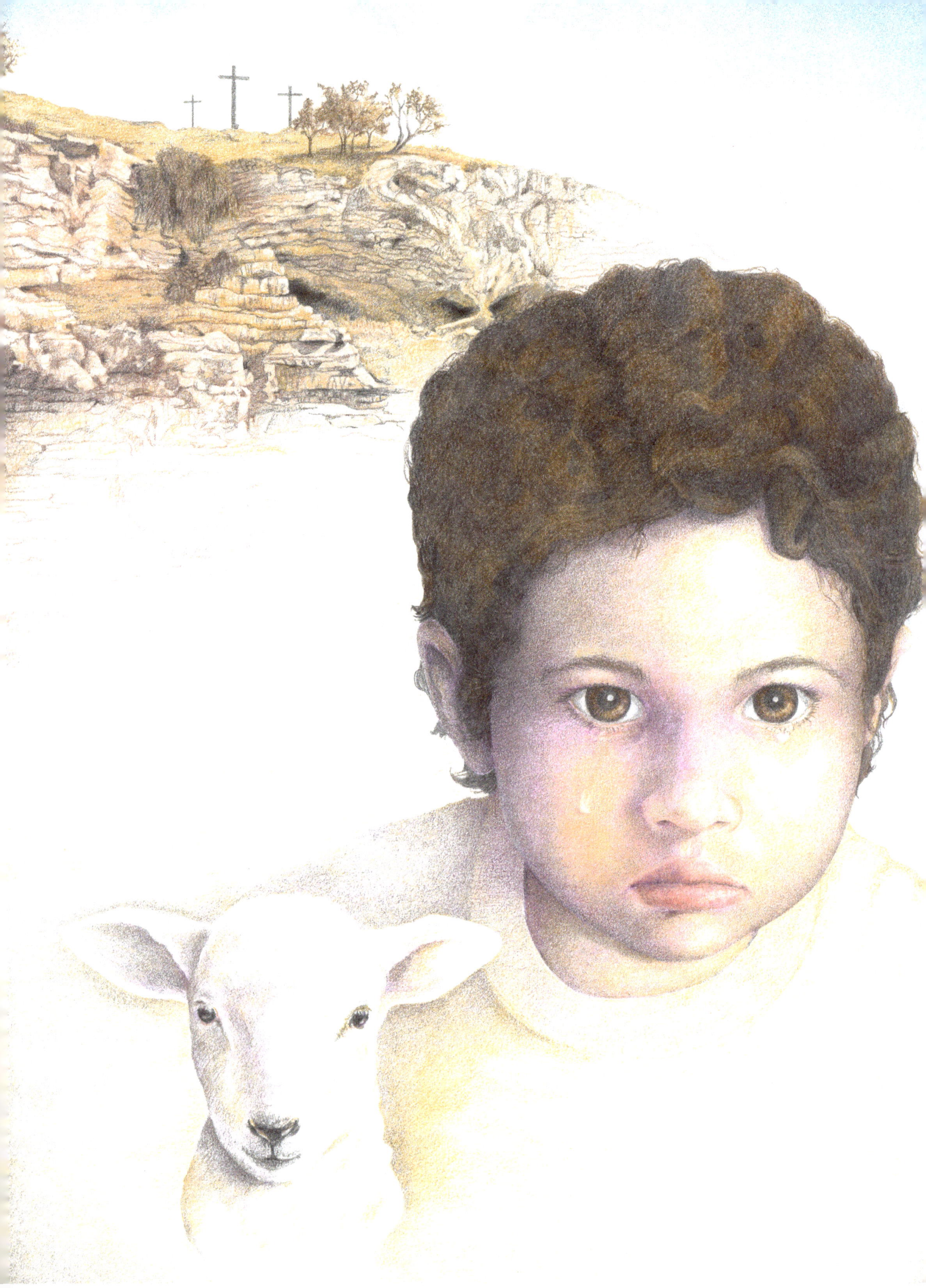

Jesus is the Lamb of God;

my sin He takes away;

Light of the world is He;

He turns my night to day.

The Lord of lords will rule the earth

in truth and righteousness;

Before Him every knee will bow

and every tongue confess.

The next day he [John] saw Jesus coming toward him, and said, "Behold, the Lamb of God, who takes away the sin of the world!" John 1:29.

You know that he appeared to take away sins, and in him there is no sin. I John 3:5.

Again, Jesus spoke to them, saying, "I am the light of the world. Whoever follows me will not walk in darkness, but will have the light of life." John 8:12.

On his robe and on his thigh he has a name written, King of kings and Lord of lords. Revelation 19:16.

Therefore God has highly exalted him and bestowed on him the name that is above every name, that at the name of Jesus every knee should bow in heaven and on earth and under the earth, and every tongue confess that Jesus Christ is Lord, to the glory of God the Father. Philippians 2:9-11.

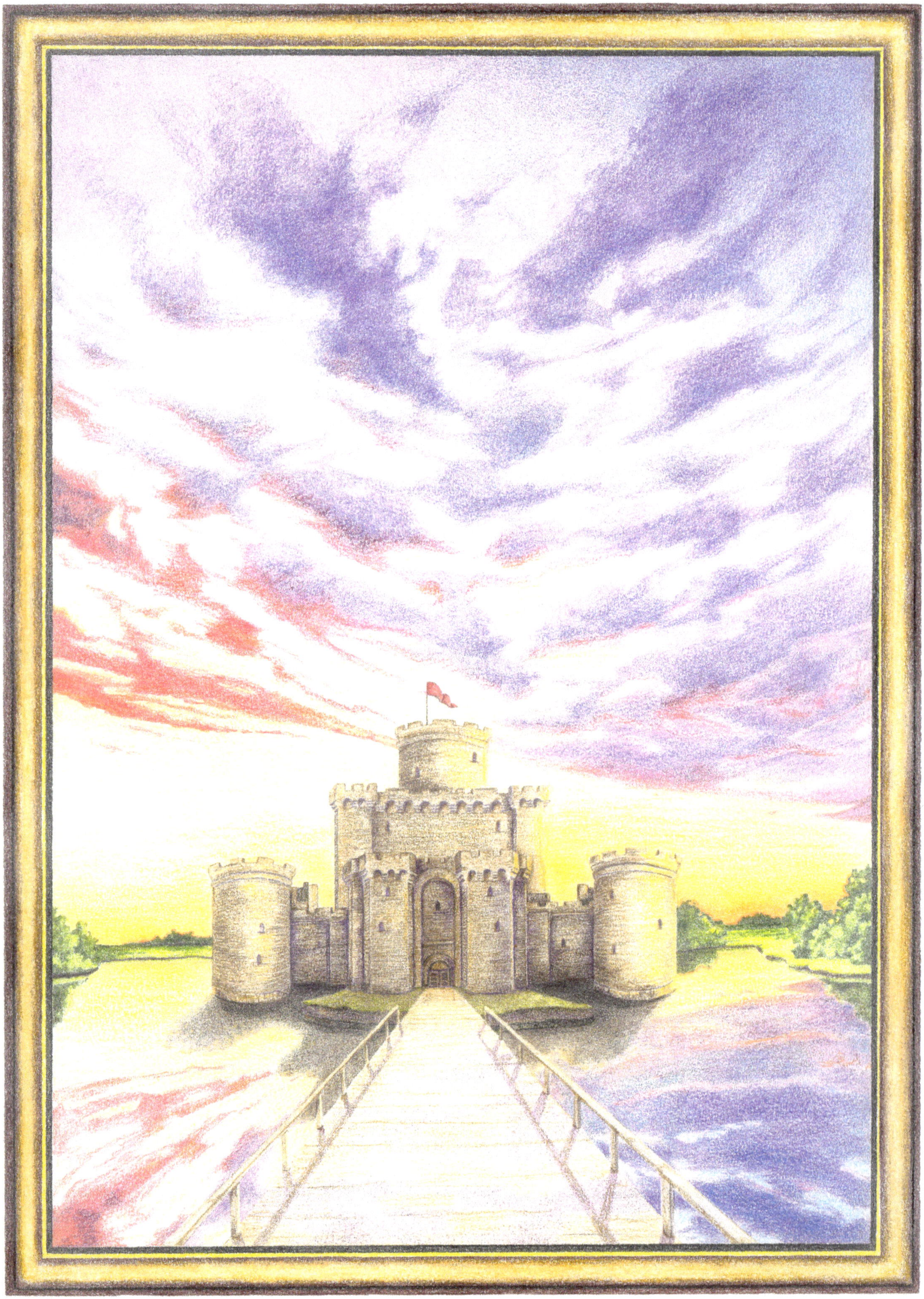

My Savior is the Mighty God;
He has all strength and power.
Nothing is too hard for Him,
my fortress and my tower.
Messiah means He is the Christ –
Prophet, Priest, and King.
Jesus loves me, this I know;
His praise I love to sing.

For to us a child is born, to us a son is given; and the government shall be upon his shoulder, and his name shall be called, Wonderful Counselor, Mighty God, Everlasting Father, Prince of Peace. Isaiah 9:6.

Ah, Lord God! It is you who have made the heavens and the earth by your great power and by your outstretched arm! Nothing is too hard for you. Jeremiah 32:17.

The LORD is my rock and my fortress and my deliverer; my God, my rock in whom I take refuge, my shield, and the horn of my salvation, my stronghold. Psalms 18:2.

The woman said to him, "I know that Messiah is coming (he who is called Christ). When he comes, he will tell us all things." Jesus said to her, "I who speak to you am he." John 4:25-26

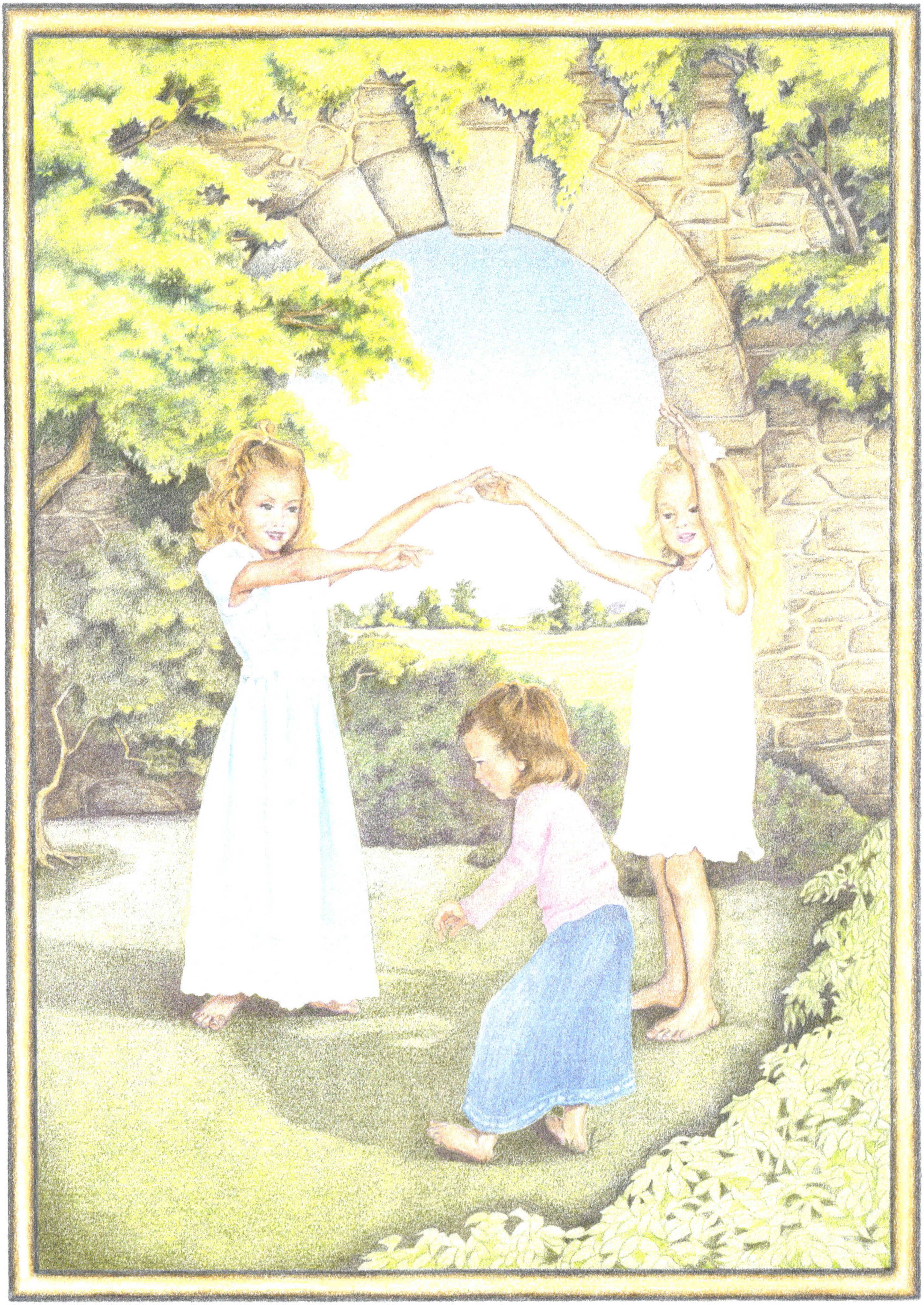

He was called a Nazarene,
from Nazareth, you see;
There Jesus lived and worked and played,
a little child like me.

And he [Joseph] went and lived in a city called Nazareth, that what was spoken by the prophet might be fulfilled: "He shall be called a Nazarene." Matthew 2:23.

And Jesus increased in wisdom and in stature and in favor with God and man. Luke 2:52.

For God so loved the world... John 3:16

His **O**nly Son God gave the world
because He loves us so;
Believe, receive eternal life;
His Word says you can know.

———————

For God so loved the world that he gave his only Son, that whoever believes in him should not perish but have eternal life. John 3:16.

I [Paul] write these things to you who believe in the name of the Son of God that you may know that you have eternal life. I John 5:13.

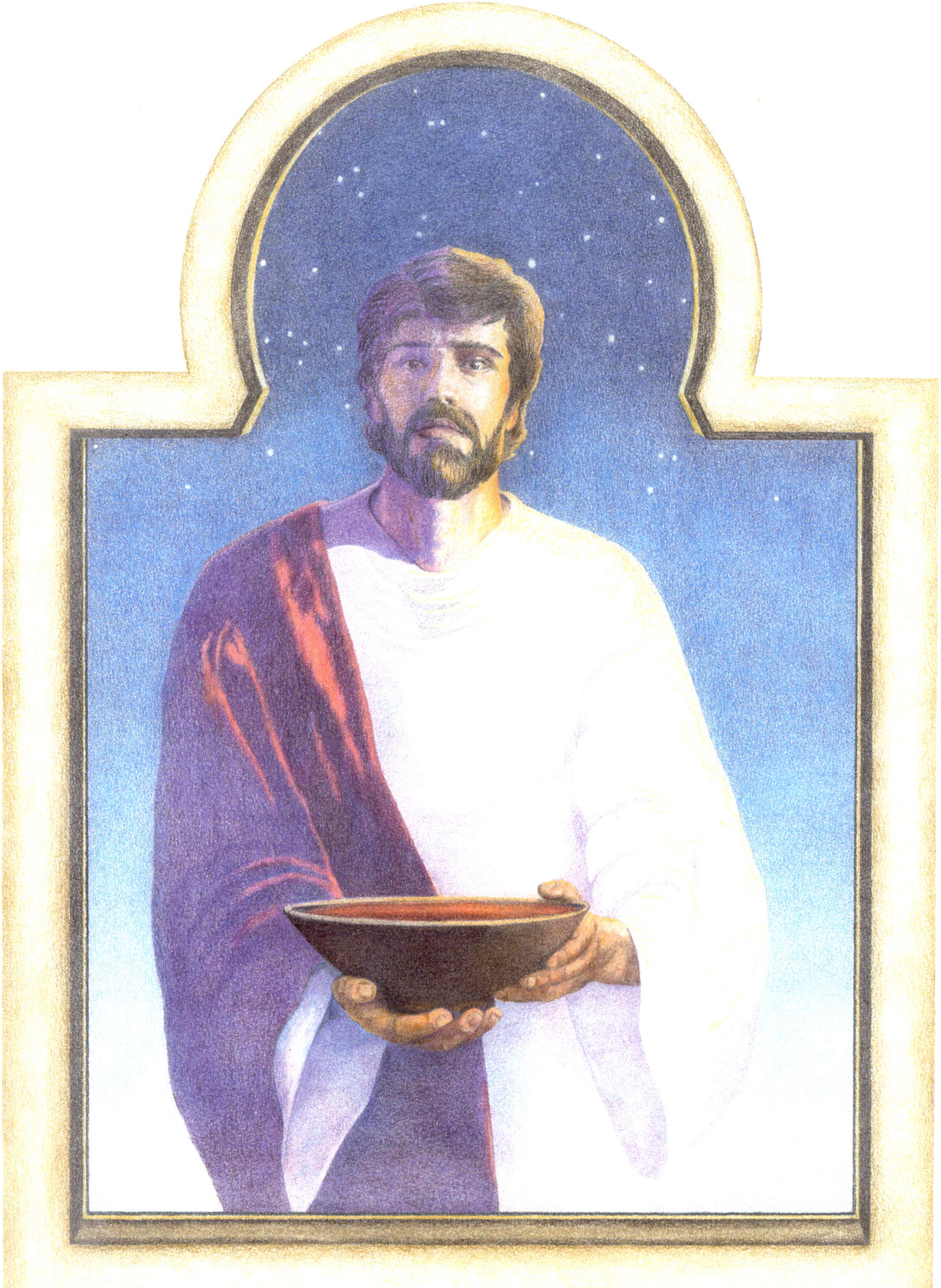

P

Jesus is my Great High Priest;

He is the Prince of Peace;

He prays for me at God's right hand;

His reign will never cease.

. . . we have a great high priest . . . Jesus, the Son of God . . . Hebrews 4:14.

. . . and his name shall be called . . . Prince of Peace. Of the increase of his government and of his peace there will be no end. Isaiah 9:6-7.

Who is to condemn? Christ Jesus is the one who died – more than that, who was raised – who is at the right hand of God, who indeed is interceding for us. Romans 8:34.

The kingdom of the world has become the kingdom of our Lord and of his Christ, and he shall reign forever and ever. Revelation 11:15.

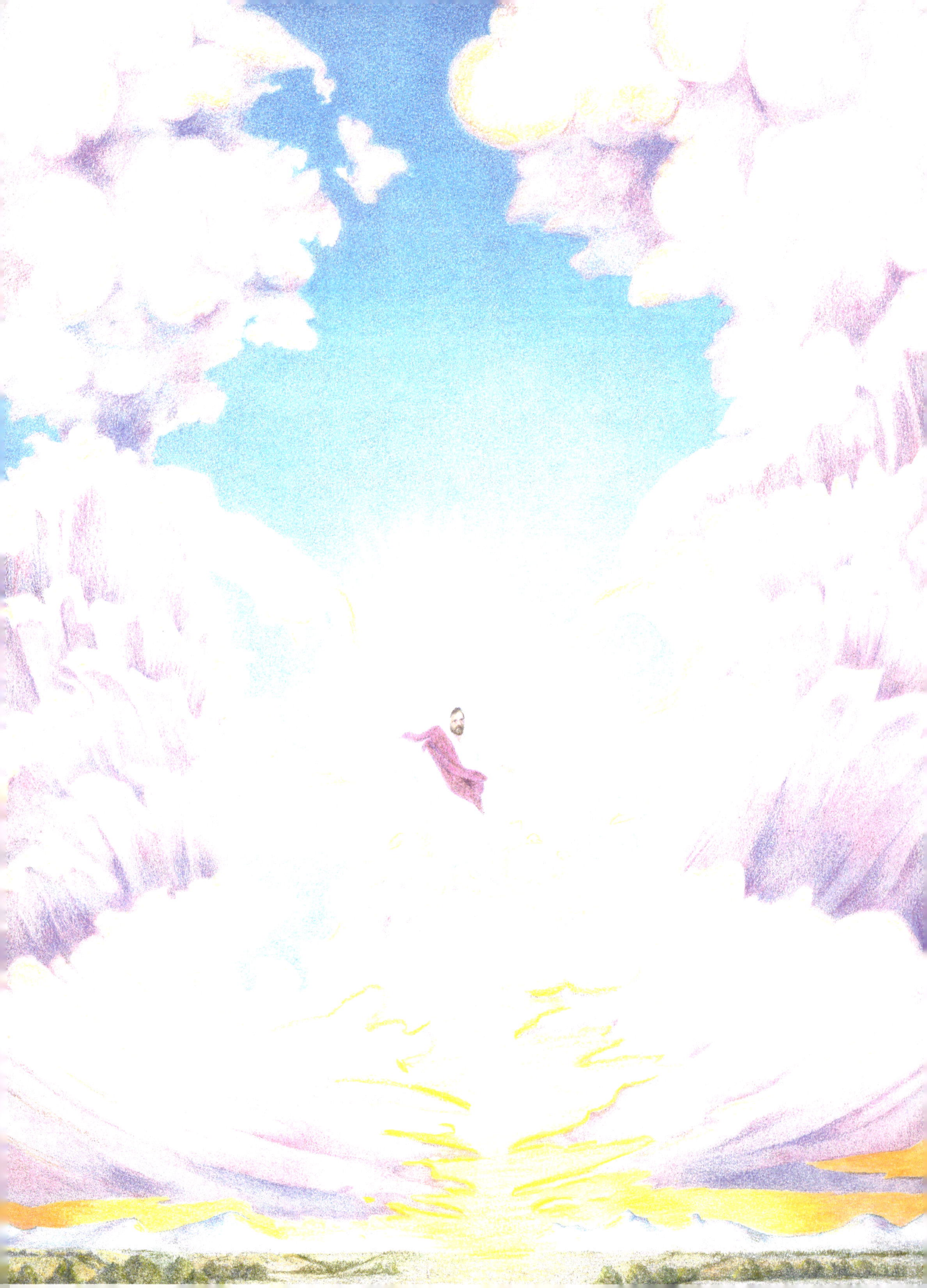

The **Q**uickly-Coming One returns;
we'll meet Him in the air;
He'll take us to His heavenly home,
to live forever there.

He who testifies to these things says, "Yes, I am coming quickly." Amen. Come, Lord Jesus. Revelation 22:20, NASV

For the Lord himself will descend from heaven with a cry of command, with the voice of an archangel, and with the sound of the trumpet of God. And the dead in Christ will rise first. Then we who are alive, who are left, will be caught up together with them in the clouds to meet the Lord in the air, and so we will always be with the Lord. I Thessalonians 4:16-17.

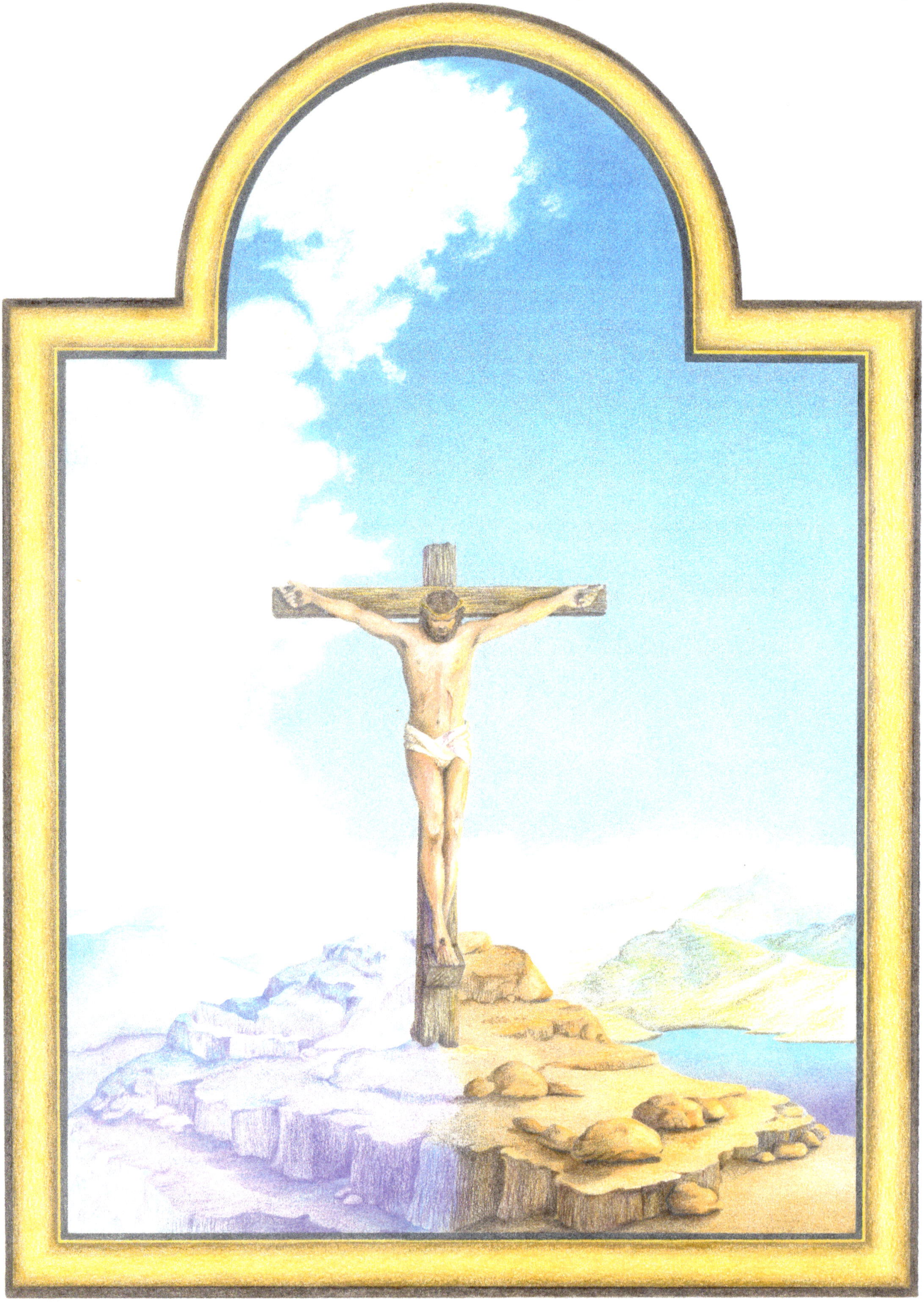

My Redeemer gave Himself;
for me He came to die;
The Resurrection and the Life;
He lives and so shall I.

Thus says the LORD, the King of Israel and his Redeemer, the LORD of hosts; I am the first and I am the last; besides me there is no God. Isaiah 44:6.

For I know that my Redeemer lives, and at the last he will stand upon the earth. Job 19:25.

In him we have redemption through his blood, the forgiveness of our trespasses, according to the riches of his grace. Ephesians 1:7.

Jesus said to her [Martha], "I am the resurrection and the life. Whoever believes in me, though he die, yet shall he live, and everyone who lives and believes in me shall never die. Do you believe this?" John 11:26

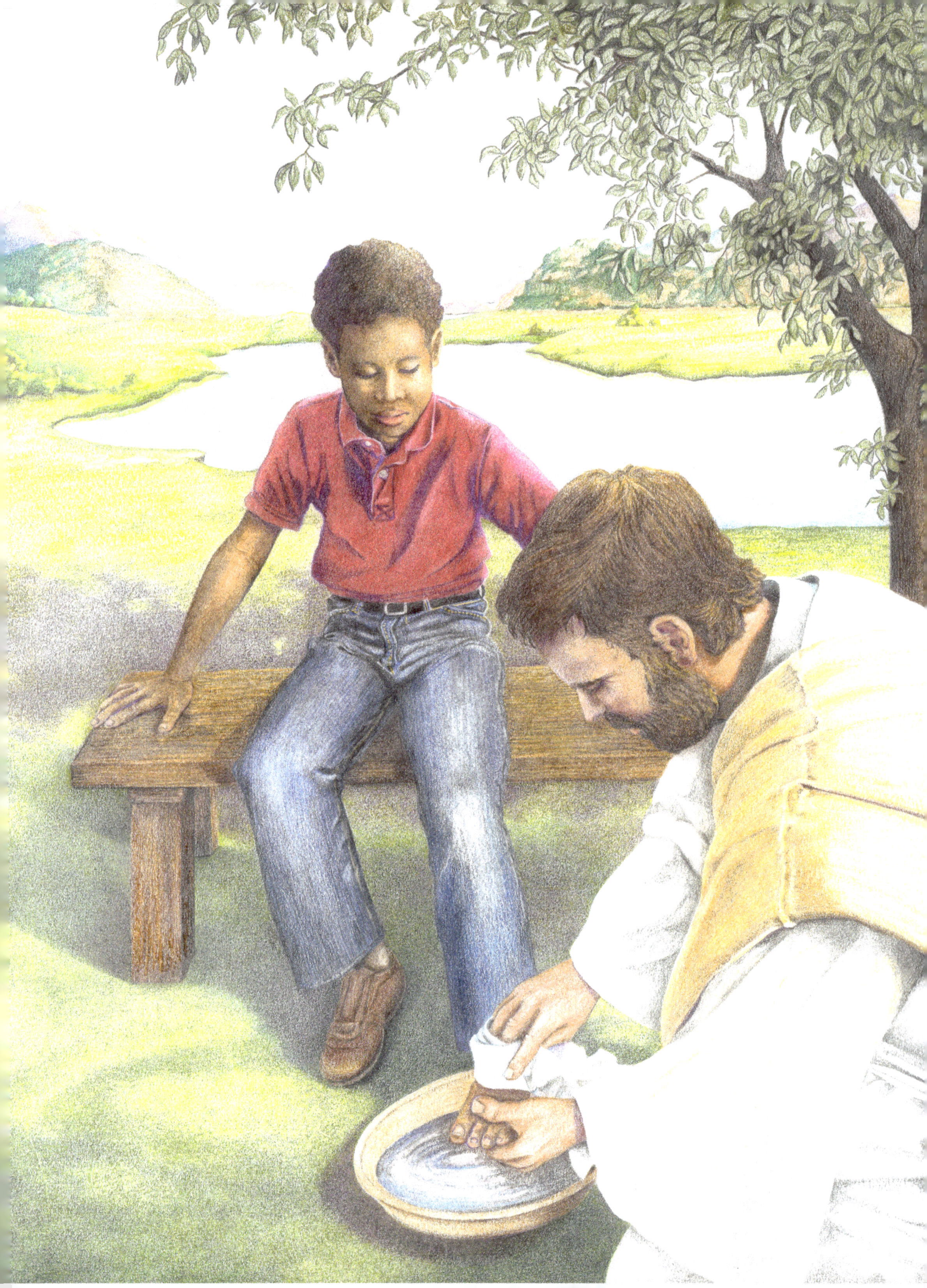

My Savior is the Son of God;
He left His heavenly throne
To suffer as a Servant meek,
that I might be His own.

———

And we have seen and testify that the Father has sent his Son to be the Savior of the world. I John 4:14.

. . . these are written so that you may believe that Jesus is the Christ, the Son of God, and that by believing you may have life in his name. John 20:31

. . . by his knowledge shall the righteous one, my servant, make many to be accounted righteous, and he shall bear their iniquities. Isaiah 53:11.

For even the Son of Man came not to be served but to serve, and to give his life as a ransom for many. Mark 10:45.

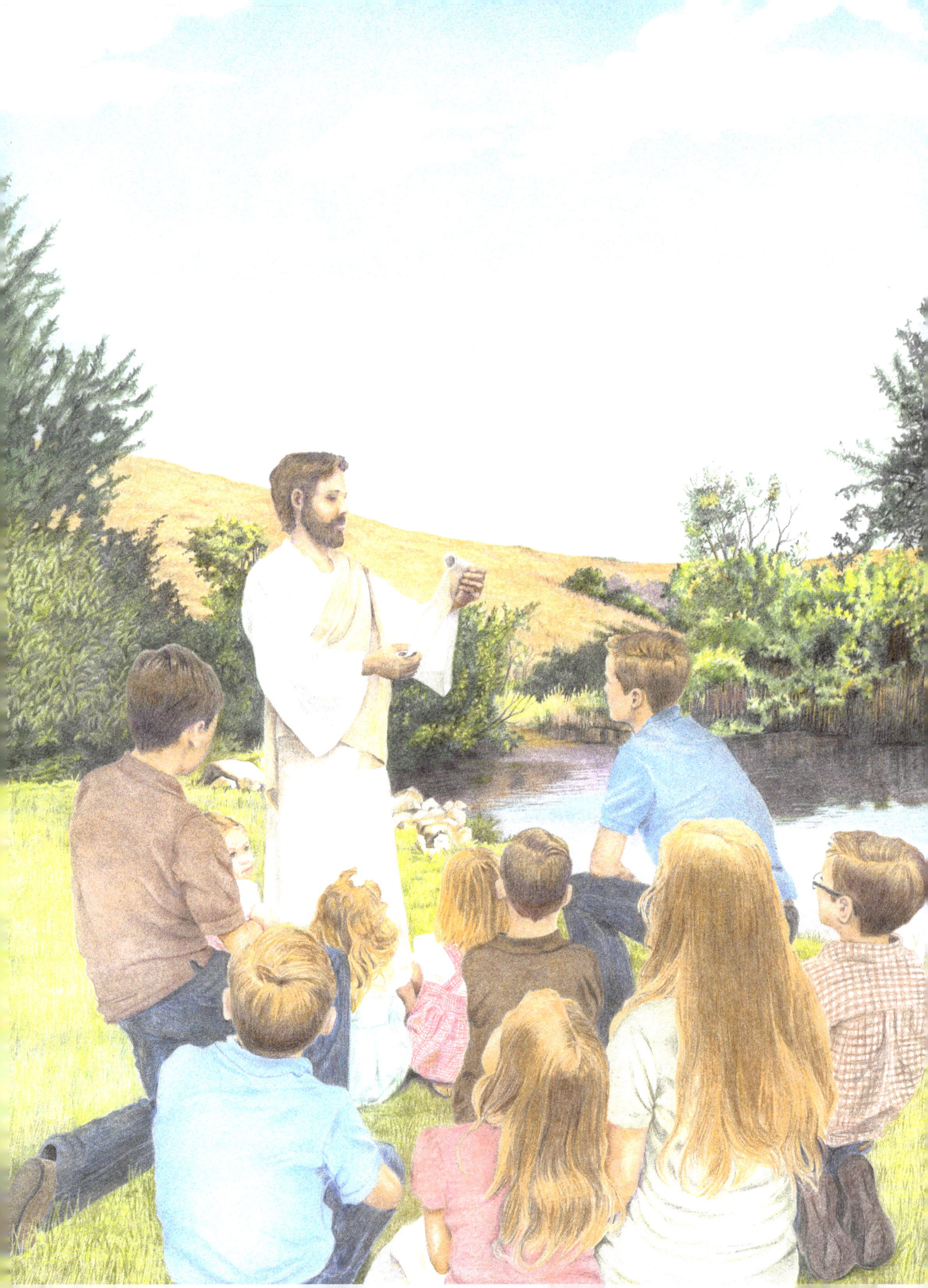

My Teacher is Himself the Truth;
His Word is right and sure.
He speaks to me the words of life;
forever they endure.

———

You call me Teacher and Lord, and you are right, for so I am. John 13:13.

Jesus said to him, "I am the way, and the truth, and the life. No one comes to the Father except through me." John 14:6.

. . . "Teacher, we know that you are true and teach the word of God truthfully . . . " Matthew 22:16.

Simon Peter answered him, "Lord, to whom shall we go? You have the words of eternal life …" John 6:68.

Heaven and earth will pass away, but my words will not pass away. Matthew 24:35.

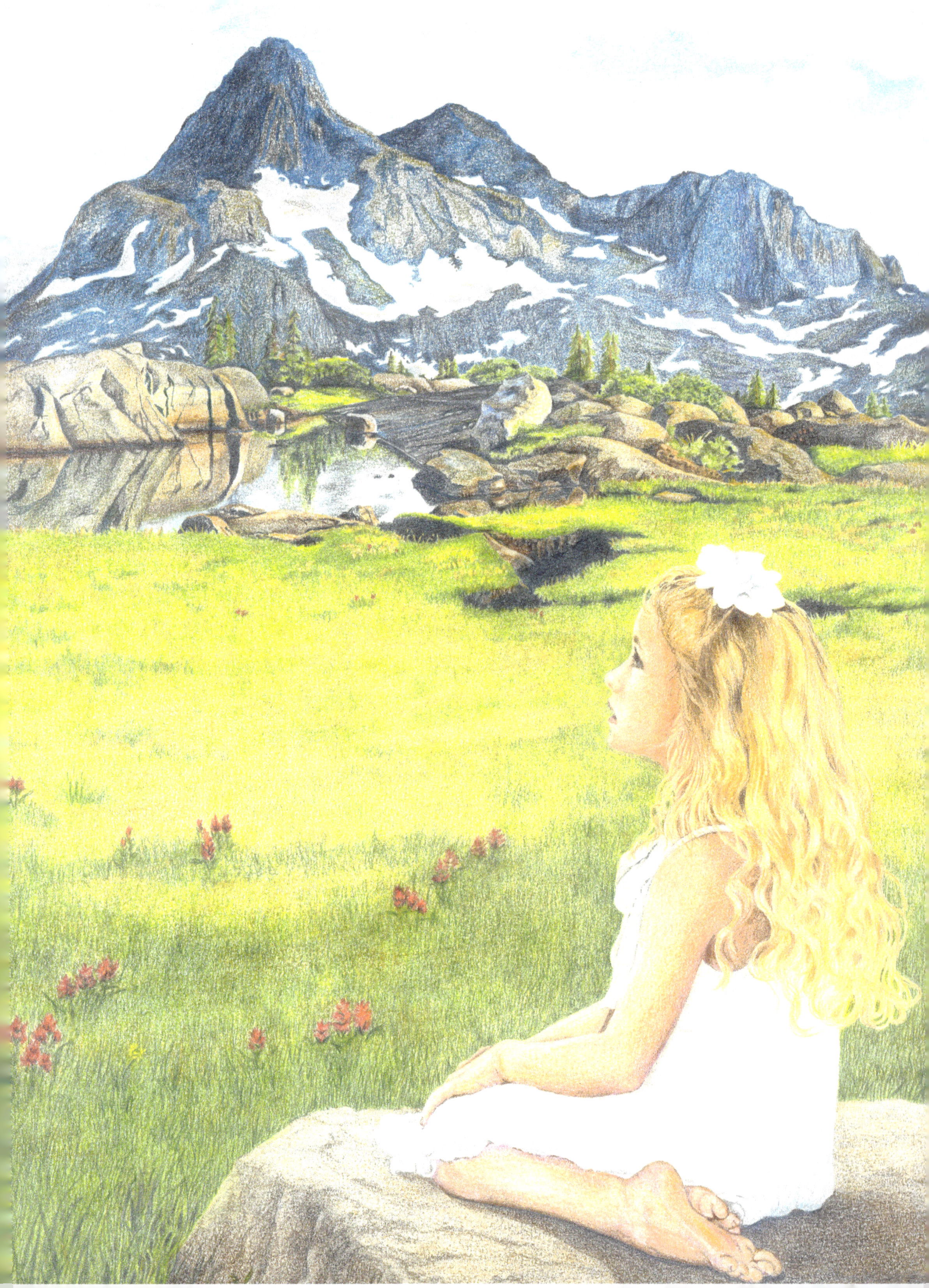

Upright is my Lord, the Christ;
in Him there is no sin;
He is my Rock, my hiding place,
and I am safe therein.

———

*. . . the LORD is upright; he is my rock, and there is no unrighteousness in him. Psalms 92:15.
You know that he appeared to take away sins, and in him there is no sin. I John 3:5*

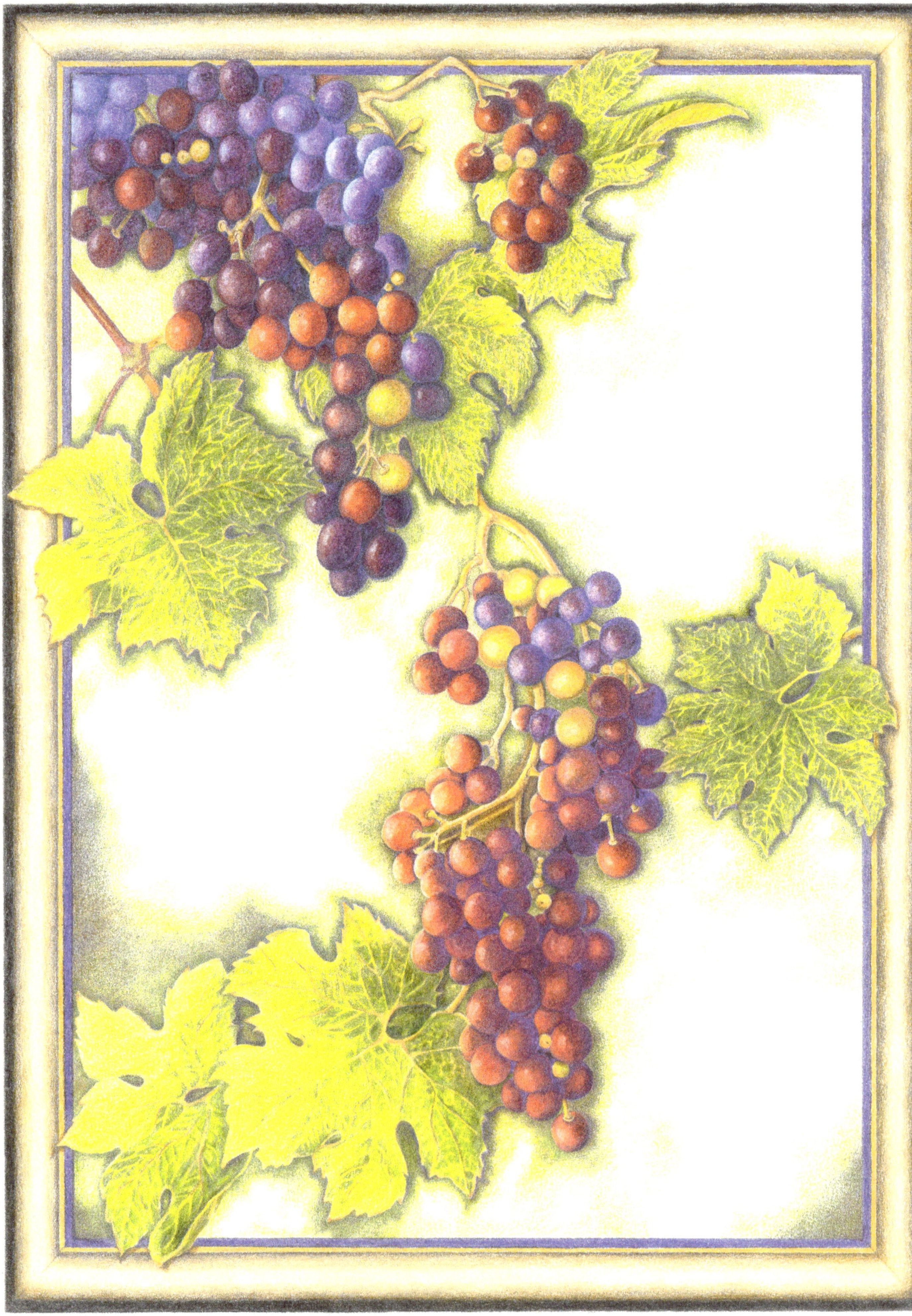

Jesus is the one true Vine,
through me His fruit to bear.
If closely I abide in Him,
He hears my every prayer.

———

I am the vine; you are the branches. Whoever abides in me and I in him, he it is that bears much fruit, for apart from me you can do nothing. John 15:5.

If you abide in me and my words abide in you, ask whatever you wish, and it will be done for you. John 15:7.

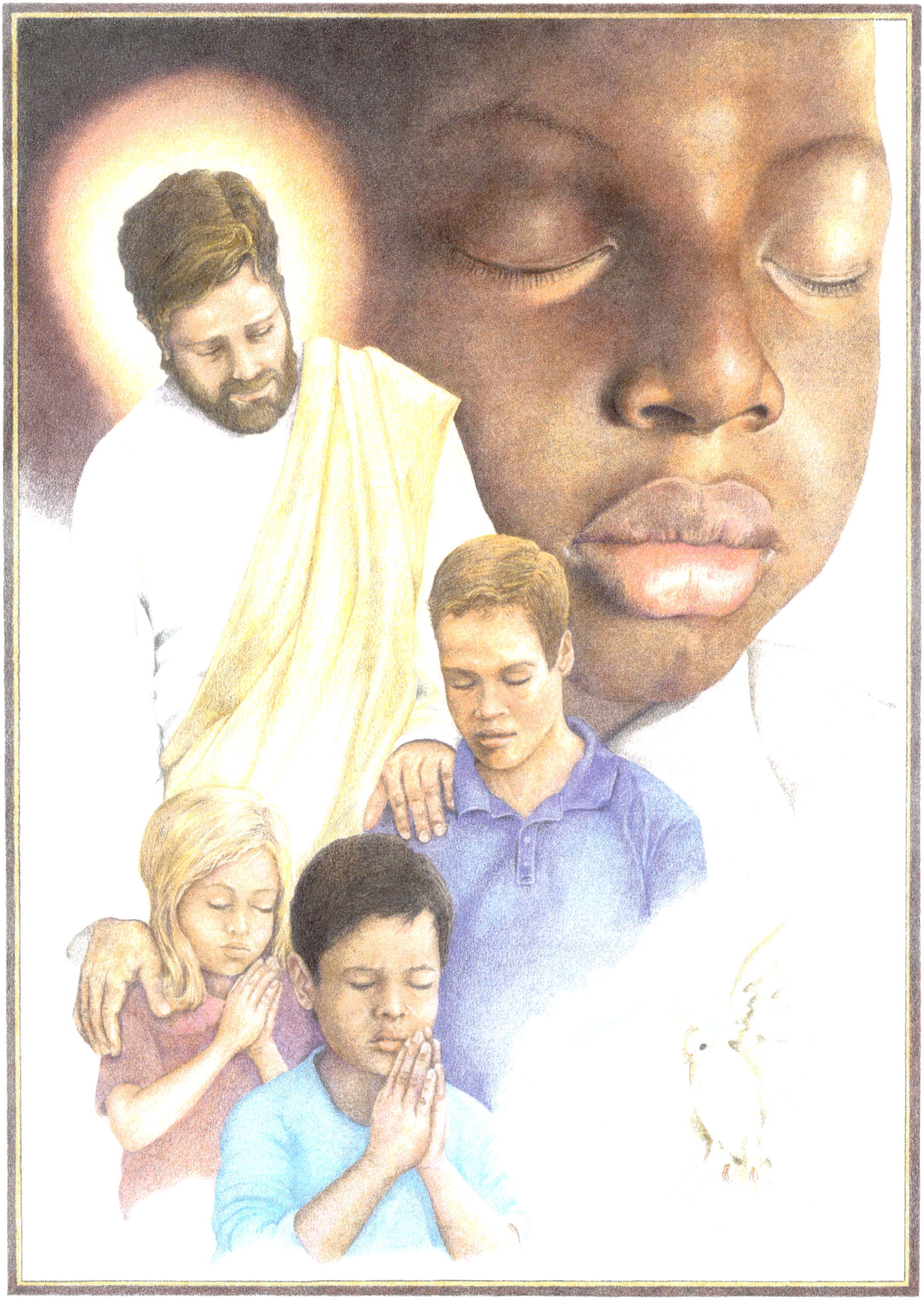

The **W**ord was God; He made all things,
full of truth and grace;
To the Father's house He is the **W**ay;
for me He makes a place.

In the beginning was the Word, and the Word was with God, and the Word was God. He was in the beginning with God. All things were made through him, and without him was not anything made that was made. John 1:1-3.

And the Word became flesh and dwelt among us, and we have seen his glory, glory as of the only Son from the Father, full of grace and truth. John 1:14.

Jesus said to him, "I am the way, and the truth, and the life. No one comes to the Father except through me." John 14:6.

In my Father's house are many rooms. If it were not so, would I have told you that I go to prepare a place for you? John 14:2-3.

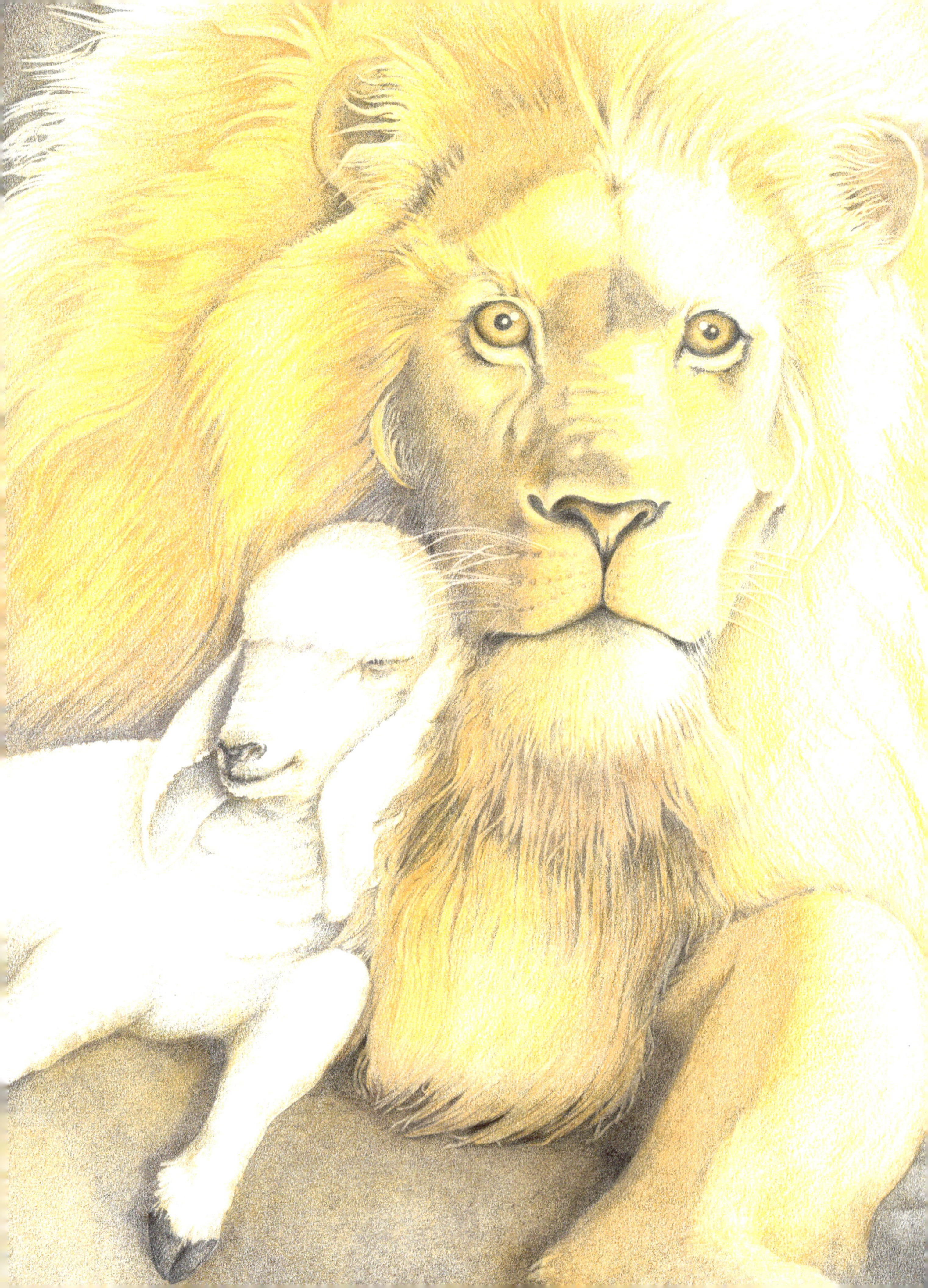

His name is eXalted above earth and heaven
higher than any other name given,
more eXcellent than names of angels so strong,
to the Lion and Lamb all praises belong.

Let them praise the name of the LORD, for his name alone is exalted; his majesty is above earth and heaven. Psalms 148:13. (see also Ps. 138:2, Isaiah 12:4)

Therefore God has highly exalted him and bestowed on him the name that is above every name. Philippians 2:9.

. . . After making purification for sins, he sat down at the right hand of the majesty on high, having become as much superior to angels as the name he has inherited is more excellent than theirs. Hebrews 1:3-4.

. . . the Lion of the tribe of Judah, the Root of David, has conquered. Revelation 5:5.

. . . Worthy is the Lamb who was slain, to receive power and wealth and wisdom and might and honor and glory and blessing! Revelation 5:12.

בָּרוּךְ אַתָּה יְיָ, אֱלֹהֵינוּ מֶלֶךְ הָעוֹלָם, אֲשֶׁר קִדְּשָׁנוּ בְּמִצְוֹתָיו, וְצִוָּנוּ לְהִתְעַטֵּף כַּצִיצִת:

Yahweh means "Jehovah, Lord",
His name from ancient days;
God Himself in human form,
worthy of all praise!

That they may know that you alone, whose name is the Lord, are the Most High over all the earth. Psalms 83:18.

In the beginning was the Word, and the Word was with God, and the Word was God. John 1:1

Note: The ancient Hebrews regarded the name of God, YHWH (no vowels) so sacred they would not dare pronounce it when reading aloud the Old Testament for fear of violating the third commandment. So they substituted the title "Adonai" which is translated "Lord" (small capital letters) in English versions.

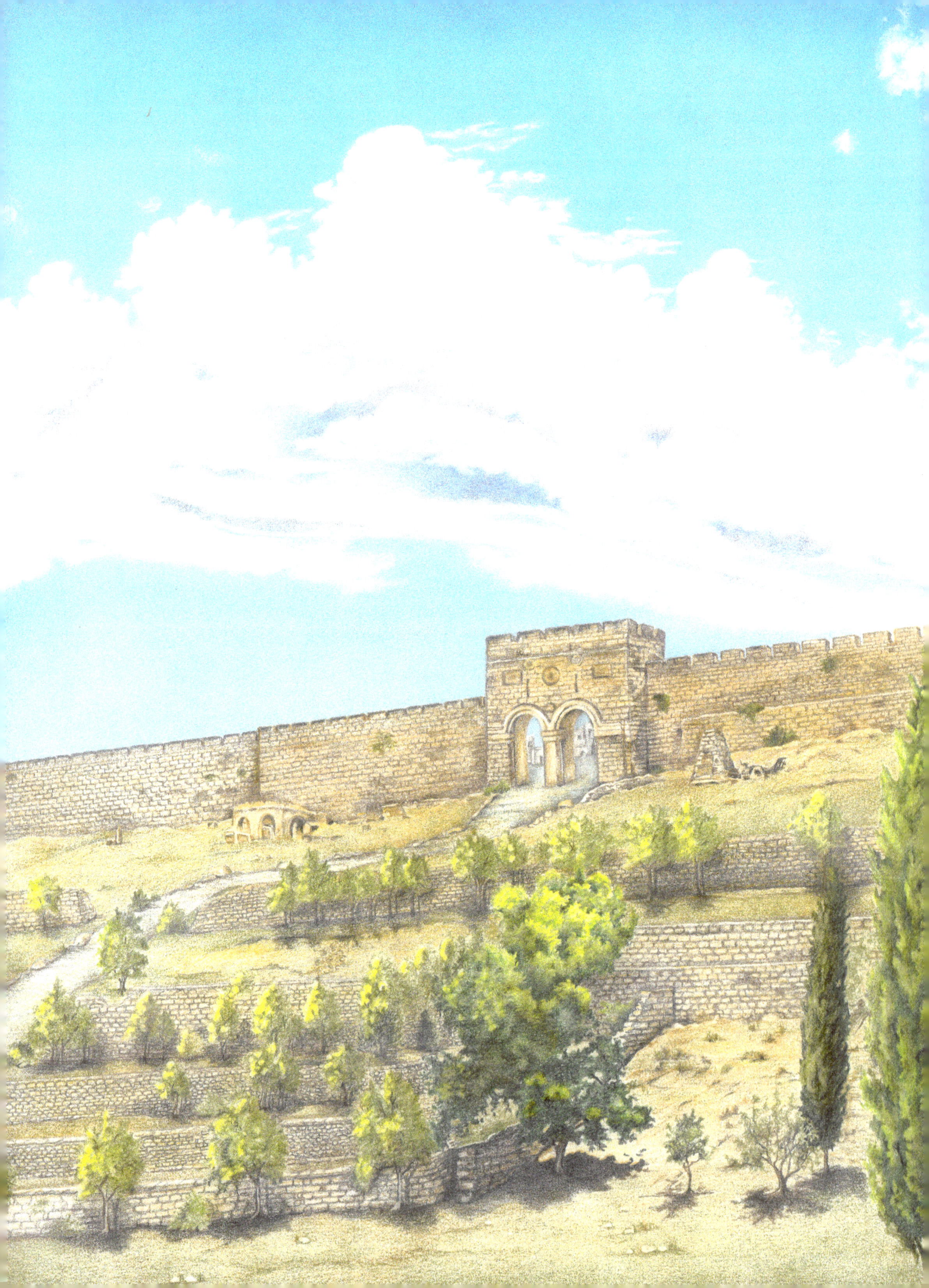

Zion's Redeemer came for me
because He loved me so;
His blood has paid for all my sin;
He's coming back – I know!

"And a Redeemer will come to Zion, to those in Jacob who turn from transgression," declared the LORD. Isaiah 59:20.

. . . Christ, having been offered once to bear the sins of many, will appear a second time, not to deal with sin but to save those who are eagerly waiting for him. Hebrews 9:28.

Note: Although "Zion" can have several different meanings, it usually refers to the city of Jerusalem.

About the Author

Steve Newby is employed on a Kansas grain and cattle farm. He is a husband, father of four, and grandfather. One of his favorite Bible passages is Ephesians 2:1-10. Verses 4 and 5 say, "But God, being rich in mercy, because of the great love with which he loved us, even when we were dead in our trespasses, made us alive together with Christ– by grace you have been saved."

About the Illustrator

From early childhood, Carolyn (Hadduck) Holmes remembers being interested in art, spending many hours sketching. Primarily fascinated with the human face, her first serious attempt was a pencil drawing of Abraham Lincoln when she was eight. Being privileged to have many good art teachers in the early years added knowledge, inspiration, and encouragement to her growth as an artist.

Holmes graduated from Emporia State University earning a Bachelor of Fine Arts degree with an emphasis in pottery. Despite varied exposure to other art mediums she never lost sight of her love for drawing. Currently, young children and the elderly is most often her subject of choice. Oil painting was not pursued until she was in her fifties, having first completed the raising of five children. With the empty nest has come more time to focus on her interests in art. For this book's illustrations Holmes has used oil pencils.

Carolyn Holmes resides in Tribune, Kansas with her husband Stuart where she pursues portrait painting. Though she derives much joy from artistic pursuits her greatest fulfillment comes from her Christian faith and the fellowship she enjoys with other Christians.

Email: scholmes25@gmail.com

Appendix

Some Names and Descriptive Titles of Christ

Advocate – I John 2:1

All and in All – Colossians 3:11

Almighty – Revelation 1:8

Alpha and Omega – Revelation 1:8; 21:6; 22:13

Amen – Revelation 3:14

Apostle and High Priest of our Confession – Hebrews 3:1

Arm of the LORD – Isaiah 53:1

Author of Life – Acts 3:15

Author and Perfector of our Faith—Hebrews 12:2

Author (or Founder) of Salvation – Hebrews 2:10

Awesome in Glorious Deeds – Exodus 15:11

Beginning and End – Revelation 21:6; 22:13

Beginning [Beginner] of Creation – Revelation 3:14, Colossians 1:15-18

Beloved — Ephesians 1:6

Beloved Son – Matthew 3:17; 17:5; John 12:28

Blessed and Only Sovereign – I Timothy 6:15

Branch –Zechariah 6:12

Branch of Righteousness – Jeremiah 33:15

Bread of God – John 6:33

Bread of Life – John 6:35, 48

Bright and Morning Star – Revelation 22:16

Chief Shepherd — Peter 5:4

Chosen of God – Luke 23:35; Isaiah 43:10

Christ – John 21:31; over 500 others

Cornerstone – Acts 4:11; Ephesians 2:20; I Peter 2:7

Creator – John 1:3; Colossians 1:16; Hebrews 1:2

Dayspring – Luke 1:78

Daystar – II Peter 1:19

Desire of All Nations – Haggai 2:7

Deliverer – Romans 11:26

Doer of Wonders – Exodus 15:11

Door – John 10:9

Ensign [Signal] of the People – Isaiah 11:10

Eternal Life – I John 1:2; 5:20

Everlasting Father – Isaiah 9:6

Excellency of God – Isaiah 35:1-2

Faithful and True – Revelation 19:11

Faithful Witness – Revelation 1:5

Faithful and True Witness – Revelation 3:14

First and Last – Revelation 1:17; 2:8; 22:13

Firstborn – Romans 8:29

Firstborn from the Dead – Revelation 1:5

Firstfruits – II Corinthians 15:20

Forerunner – Hebrews 6:20

Foundation – I Corinthians 3:11

Friend of Sinners – Luke 7:34

Fullness of God – Colossians 1:19; 2:9

Gift of God – Isaiah 9:6; John 3:16; Romans 8:32

Glory of God – John 1:14; II Corinthians 4:6

God – John 1:1; 20:28; Hebrews 1:8 (from Psalms 45:6-7); 2 Peter 1:1; others

Good Shepherd – John 10:11, 14
Good Teacher – Matthew 19:16
Great God and Savior – Titus 2:13
Great Shepherd – Hebrews 13:20
Great High Priest – Hebrews 4:14

Head of the Church – Ephesians 1:22; 4:15; 5:23; Colossians 1:18
Heir of All Things – Hebrews 1:2
Helper – Hebrews 13:5-6
High Priest – Hebrews 2:17; 6:19-20
Holy and True – Revelation 3:7
Holy One – Acts 3:14
Hope – I Timothy 1:1
Hope of Israel – Jeremiah 14:8; 17:13; Acts 28:20
Hope of Glory – Colossians 1:27
Horn of Salvation – Luke 1:69

I Am – John 5:58
Image of God – 2 Corinthians 4:4; Hebrews 1:3
Immanuel – Isaiah 7:14; Matthew 1:23

Jehovah – Isaiah 44:6
Jesus – Matthew 1:21
Jesus Christ – Romans 1:4 (over 950 references to Jesus, Jesus Christ, Christ Jesus)

King Eternal – I Timothy 1:17
King of the Ages – Revelation 15:3
King of Glory – Psalms 24:7-8
King of Heaven – Daniel 4:37
King of Israel – John 1:49
King of the Jews – Matthew 2:2; 27:11
King of kings – I Timothy 6:15; Revelation 19:16

Lamb – Revelation 13:8

Lamb of God – John 1:29

Lamb Without Blemish or Spot – I Peter 1:19

Last Adam – I Corinthians 15:45

Life – John 14:6; Colossians 3:4

Light of the World – John 8:12

Lion of the Tribe of Judah – Revelation 5:5

Living One – Revelation 1:18

Living Stone – I Peter 2:4

Lord – Luke 2:11, John 13:13; 20:28, hundreds more

Lord and Savior – II Peter 1:11

LORD our Righteousness – Jeremiah 23:6

Majestic in Holiness – Exodus 15:11

Man Christ Jesus – I Timothy 2:5

Man from Heaven – I Corinthians 15:48

Man of Sorrows – Isaiah 53:3

Mediator – I Timothy 2:5

Mediator of the New Covenant – Hebrews 9:15

Merciful and Faithful High Priest – Hebrews 2:17

Messenger of the Covenant – Malachi 3:1

Messiah – John 1:41; 4:25

Messiah the Prince – Daniel 9:25

Mighty God – Isaiah 9:6

Morning Star – Revelation 22:16

Offering – Ephesians 5:2

Offspring of David – Revelation 22:16

Only Begotten Son of God – John 1:18; 3:16, I John 4:9

Only Son of the Father – John 1:14

Only Wise God – I Timothy 1:17

Our Great God and Savior – Titus 2:13

Our Passover Lamb – I Corinthians 5:7

Our Peace – Ephesians 2:14

Our Redemption – I Corinthians 1:30

Our Righteousness – I Corinthians 1:30

Our Sanctification (Holiness) – I Corinthians 1:30

Passover Lamb – I Corinthians 5:7

Power of God – I Corinthians 1:24

Precious Cornerstone – I Peter 2:6

Priest – Hebrews 5:6; 7:17

Prince of Peace – Isaiah 9:6

Prophet – Acts 3:22

Propitiation for Our Sins – I John 2:2; 4:10, Romans 3:25 (Full, sufficient, satisfactory sacrifice or payment)

Rabbi (Teacher) – John 1:49

Radiance of the Glory of God – Hebrews 1:3

Redeemer – Job 19:25; Isaiah 44:6; 59:20; 60:16

Resurrection and Life – John 11:25

Righteous Branch – Jeremiah 23:5

Righteous One – Acts 7:52; I John 2:1

Rock – I Corinthians 10:4

Root of David – Revelation 5:5; 22:16

Root of Jesse – Isaiah 11:10

Ruler of Kings on Earth – Revelation 1:5

Ruler Over the Nations – Psalms 22:28

Sacrifice – Ephesians 5:2

Savior – Ephesians 5:23; Titus 1:4; 3:6; 2 Peter 2:20

Savior of the World – John 4:42

Servant – Isaiah 42:1-4; 52:13; 53:11; Matthew 12:18; Acts 3:13,26; 4:27,30

Son of David – Luke 18:39

Son of God – Matthew 14:33; 16:16; 27:54; Mark 1:1; Luke 1:35; John 1:34,49; 3:18; 20:31, Romans 1:3-4; Hebrews 4;14

Son of Man – Matthew 8:20, many others

Son of the Most High God – Luke 1:32

Source of Eternal Salvation – Hebrews 5:9

Stone the Builders Rejected – Acts 4:11; I Peter 2:7

Teacher — John 13:13

True Bread – John 6:32

True God – I John 6:32

True Light – John 1:9

True Vine – John 15:1

Truth – John 1:14; 14:6

Way – John 14:6

Wisdom of God – I Corinthians 1:24

Wonderful Counselor – Isaiah 9:6

Word of God – Revelation 19:13

Note: Most of these names and titles come from personal study. Some were taken from the five-volume series on the names of Christ by Dr. Charles J. Rolls.

Rolls, Charles J. *The Indescribable Christ; Names and Titles of Jesus Christ A – G.* Loizeaux Brothers. Neptune, New Jersey. 1953, 1983.

Rolls, Charles J. *The World's Greatest Name; Names and Title of Jesus Christ H – K.* Loizeaux Brothers. Neptune, New Jersey. 1956, 1984, 1989.

Rolls, Charles J. *Time's Noblest Name; Names and Titles of Jesus Christ L – O.* Loizeaux Brothers. Neptune, New Jersey. 1958, 1985, 1988.

Rolls, Charles J. *The Name Above Every Name; Names and Titles of Jesus Christ P – S.* Loizeaux Brothers. Neptune, New Jersey. 1965, 1985.

Rolls, Charles J. *His Glorious Name; Names and Titles of Jesus Christ T – Z.* Loizeaux Brothers. Neptune, New Jersey. 1975, 1985.

CPSIA information can be obtained
at www.ICGtesting.com
Printed in the USA
LVHW021001211120
672134LV00011B/783